MAX LUCADO

LIFE LESSONS *from*

1, 2, 3 JOHN
AND JUDE

Living and Loving by Truth

PREPARED BY THE LIVINGSTONE CORPORATION

THOMAS NELSON
Since 1798

Published in Nashville, Tennessee, by Thomas Nelson. Thomas Nelson is a registered trademark of HarperCollins Christian Publishing, Inc.

Produced with the assistance of the Livingstone Corporation. Project staff include Jake Barton, Joel Bartlett, Andy Culbertson, Mary Horner Collins, Will Reaves, and Rachel Hawkins.

Editor: Len Woods

All Scripture quotations, unless otherwise indicated, are taken from The Holy Bible, New International Version®, NIV®. Copyright © 1973, 1978, 1984, 2011 by Biblica, Inc.™ Used by permission. All rights reserved worldwide. www.Zondervan.com. The "NIV" and "New International Version" are trademarks registered in the United States Patent and Trademark Office by Biblica, Inc.®

Scripture quotations marked NKJV are taken from the New King James Version®. Copyright © 1982 by Thomas Nelson. Used by permission. All rights reserved.

Scripture quotations marked TJB are taken from *The Jerusalem Bible* © 1966 by Darton Longman & Todd Ltd and Doubleday and Company Ltd.

Material for the "Inspiration" sections taken from the following books:

3:16: The Numbers of Hope. © 2007 by Max Lucado. Thomas Nelson, a registered trademark of HarperCollins Christian Publishing, Inc., Nashville, Tennessee.

And the Angels Were Silent. Copyright © 2004 by Max Lucado. Thomas Nelson, a registered trademark of HarperCollins Christian Publishing, Inc., Nashville, Tennessee.

Because of Bethlehem. Copyright © 2016 by Max Lucado. Thomas Nelson, a registered trademark of HarperCollins Christian Publishing, Inc., Nashville, Tennessee.

Come Thirsty. Copyright © 2004 by Max Lucado. Thomas Nelson, a registered trademark of HarperCollins Christian Publishing, Inc., Nashville, Tennessee.

Fearless. © 2009 by Max Lucado. Thomas Nelson, a registered trademark of HarperCollins Christian Publishing, Inc., Nashville, Tennessee.

A Gentle Thunder. Copyright © 1995 by Max Lucado. Thomas Nelson, a registered trademark of HarperCollins Christian Publishing, Inc., Nashville, Tennessee.

The Great House of God. Copyright © 1997 by Max Lucado. Thomas Nelson, a registered trademark of HarperCollins Christian Publishing, Inc., Nashville, Tennessee.

In the Grip of Grace. Copyright © 1996 by Max Lucado. Thomas Nelson, a registered trademark of HarperCollins Christian Publishing, Inc., Nashville, Tennessee.

It's Not About Me. Copyright © 2004 by Max Lucado. Thomas Nelson, a registered trademark of HarperCollins Christian Publishing, Inc., Nashville, Tennessee.

A Love Worth Giving. Copyright © 2002 by Max Lucado. Thomas Nelson, a registered trademark of HarperCollins Christian Publishing, Inc., Nashville, Tennessee.

Just Like Jesus. Copyright © 1998 by Max Lucado. Thomas Nelson, a registered trademark of HarperCollins Christian Publishing, Inc., Nashville, Tennessee.

ISBN-13: 978-0-3100-8664-2

CONTENTS

HOW TO STUDY THE BIBLE

The Bible is a peculiar book. Words crafted in another language. Deeds done in a distant era. Events recorded in a far-off land. Counsel offered to a foreign people. It is a peculiar book.

It's surprising that anyone reads it. It's too old. Some of its writings date back 5,000 years. It's too bizarre. The book speaks of incredible floods, fires, earthquakes, and people with supernatural abilities. It's too radical. The Bible calls for undying devotion to a carpenter who called himself God's Son.

Logic says this book shouldn't survive. Too old, too bizarre, too radical.

The Bible has been banned, burned, scoffed, and ridiculed. Scholars have mocked it as foolish. Kings have branded it as illegal. A thousand times over the grave has been dug and the dirge has begun, but somehow the Bible never stays in the grave. Not only has it survived, but it has also thrived. It is the single most popular book in all of history. It has been the bestselling book in the world for years!

There is no way on earth to explain it. Which perhaps is the only explanation. For the Bible's durability is not found on *earth* but in *heaven*. The millions who have tested its claims and claimed its promises know there is but one answer: the Bible is God's book and God's voice.

As you read it, you would be wise to give some thought to two questions: *What is the purpose of the Bible?* and *How do I study the Bible?* Time spent reflecting on these two issues will greatly enhance your Bible study.

What is the purpose of the Bible?

Let the Bible itself answer that question: *"From infancy you have known the Holy Scriptures, which are able to make you wise for salvation through faith in Christ Jesus"* (2 Timothy 3:15).

The purpose of the Bible? Salvation. God's highest passion is to get his children home. His book, the Bible, describes his plan of salvation. The purpose of the Bible is to proclaim God's plan and passion to save his children.

This is the reason why this book has endured through the centuries. It dares to tackle the toughest questions about life: *Where do I go after I die? Is there a God? What do I do with my fears?* The Bible is the treasure map that leads to God's highest treasure—eternal life.

But how do you study the Bible? Countless copies of Scripture sit unread on bookshelves and nightstands simply because people don't know how to read it. What can you do to make the Bible real in your life?

The clearest answer is found in the words of Jesus: *"Ask and it will be given to you; seek and you will find; knock and the door will be opened to you"* (Matthew 7:7).

The first step in understanding the Bible is asking God to help you. You should read it prayerfully. If anyone understands God's Word, it is because of God and not the reader.

"The Advocate, the Holy Spirit, whom the Father will send in my name, will teach you all things and will remind you of everything I have said to you" (John 14:26).

Before reading the Bible, pray and invite God to speak to you. Don't go to Scripture looking for your idea, but go searching for his.

Not only should you read the Bible prayerfully, but you should also read it carefully. *"Seek and you will find"* is the pledge. The Bible is not a newspaper to be skimmed but rather a mine to be quarried. *"If you look for it as for silver and search for it as for hidden treasure, then you will understand the fear of the* LORD *and find the knowledge of God"* (Proverbs 2:4–5).

Any worthy find requires effort. The Bible is no exception. To understand the Bible, you don't have to be brilliant, but you must be willing to roll up your sleeves and search.

"Do your best to present yourself to God as one approved, a worker who does not need to be ashamed and who correctly handles the word of truth" (2 Timothy 2:15).

Here's a practical point. Study the Bible a bit at a time. Hunger is not satisfied by eating twenty-one meals in one sitting once a week. The body needs a steady diet to remain strong. So does the soul. When God sent food to his people in the wilderness, he didn't provide loaves already made. Instead, he sent them manna in the shape of *"thin flakes like frost on the ground"* (Exodus 16:14).

God gave manna in limited portions.

God sends spiritual food the same way. He opens the heavens with just enough nutrients for today's hunger. He provides *"a rule for this, a rule for that; a little here, a little there"* (Isaiah 28:10).

Don't be discouraged if your reading reaps a small harvest. Some days a lesser portion is all that is needed. What is important is to search every day for that day's message. A steady diet of God's Word over a lifetime builds a healthy soul and mind.

It's much like the little girl who returned from her first day at school feeling a bit dejected. Her mom asked, "Did you learn anything?"

"Apparently not enough," the girl responded. "I have to go back tomorrow, and the next day, and the next . . . "

Such is the case with learning. And such is the case with Bible study. Understanding comes little by little over a lifetime.

There is a third step in understanding the Bible. After the asking and seeking comes the knocking. After you ask and search, *"knock and the door will be opened to you"* (Matthew 7:7).

To knock is to stand at God's door. To make yourself available. To climb the steps, cross the porch, stand at the doorway, and volunteer. Knocking goes beyond the realm of thinking and into the realm of acting.

To knock is to ask, *What can I do? How can I obey? Where can I go?*

It's one thing to know what to do. It's another to do it. But for those who do it—those who choose to obey—a special reward awaits them.

"Whoever looks intently into the perfect law that gives freedom, and continues in it—not forgetting what they have heard, but doing it—they will be blessed in what they do" (James 1:25).

What a promise. Blessings come to those who do what they read in God's Word! It's the same with medicine. If you only read the label but ignore the pills, it won't help. It's the same with food. If you only read the recipe but never cook, you won't be fed. And it's the same with the Bible. If you only read the words but never obey, you'll never know the joy God has promised.

Ask. Search. Knock. Simple, isn't it? So why don't you give it a try? If you do, you'll see why the Bible is the most remarkable book in history.

INTRODUCTION TO
The Books of 1, 2, 3 John and Jude

1 JOHN

Tolerance. It's a prized virtue today. The ability to be understanding of those with whom you differ is a sign of sophistication.

Jesus was a champion of tolerance. He was tolerant of the disciples when they doubted. He was tolerant of the crowds when they misunderstood. He is tolerant of us when we fall.

But there is one area where Jesus was intolerant. There was one area where he was unindulgent and dogmatic. Were he to share his opinion today, he would be accused of being narrow, biased, one-sided, even bigoted.

But as far as he was concerned, when it comes to salvation, there aren't several roads . . . there is only one road. There aren't several ways . . . there is only one way. There aren't several paths . . . there is only one path. And that path is Jesus himself.

That is why it is so hard for people to believe in Jesus. It's much easier to consider him one of several options rather than *the* option. But such a philosophy is no option. Jesus closed that door. Jesus positioned himself as the peerless Savior of the world. In defining who he is, Jesus is bold and unapologetic.

His disciple John was equally firm. We first met John when he was a young man in the shadow of John the Baptist. We saw him as he stood in the shadow of the cross. We now read him as he writes as the elder statesman of the church.

John writes his first letter to dispel doubts about Jesus. False teachers have entered the church, denying the incarnation of Christ. John steps up to the bench and makes his defense. After all, John knew him, walked with him, lived with him. He saw him heal. He heard his words. John had been to the empty tomb, and he knew . . .

Jesus is not one of many options. He is the only option or nothing at all.

There are times to be tolerant. And there are times to take a stand for truth. In this letter, John takes a stand.

AUTHOR AND DATE

John, who along with Peter and James was a member of Jesus' "inner circle" of disciples. As such, he was given access to events such as the raising of Jairus' daughter (see Luke 8:49–51), Jesus' Transfiguration (see Matthew 17:1–2), and Jesus' agony in the Garden of Gethsemane (see Mark 14:32–34). Jesus referred to John and his brother, the disciple James, as "sons of thunder," perhaps due to their tendency at times to speak out like an untamed storm (see Luke 9:51–56). John, for his part, often referred to himself as "the disciple whom Jesus loved" (see John 13:23; 19:26; 21:7). It is believed James was the first disciple to be martyred, c. AD 44 (see Acts 12:2), while John was the last to die at an old age, c. AD 98. It is likely he wrote his first letter c. AD 90 from Ephesus, where he was serving as a beloved elder of the church.

SITUATION

Irenaeus, an early church father in the second century, wrote that John published his Gospel "while he was resident at Ephesus in Asia." Later, in the same work, he attributed both 1 and 2 John to the disciple as well. By the end of the second century, it was widely held that John was the author of both the Gospel and the letters that bear his name. John's audience appears to have been members of a group of churches with leaders who looked to him as their superior and patron. His purpose for writing was to combat a form of heresy that was being taught in the churches that focused on Jesus' divinity while denying his humanity. John writes to encourage the believers to endure the persecutions they are facing and not accept the false teachings of the "many antichrists [who] have come" (1 John 2:19).

KEY THEMES

- Our obedience in faith keeps us in fellowship with God.
- God will forgive our sins.
- We can measure any truth by where it places Jesus in relation to God.
- God's love and Christ's victory are the Christian's inheritance.

KEY VERSE

We proclaim to you what we have seen and heard, so that you also may have fellowship with us. And our fellowship is with the Father and with his Son, Jesus Christ (1 John 1:3).

CONTENTS

2 JOHN

The single most difficult pursuit is truth and love. That sentence is grammatically correct. I know every English teacher wants to pluralize it to read: "the most difficult pursuits are those of truth and love." But that's not what I meant to say.

True, love is a difficult pursuit. Correct, truth is a tough one too.

But put them together, pursue truth and love at the same time . . . and hang on, baby, you're in for the ride of your life.

That's the task of the Christian. Love in truth. Truth in love.

Never one at the expense of the other. Never the embrace of love without the torch of truth. Never the heat of truth without the warmth of love.

It would be easier if we could choose between the two, but we can't. So John, in his second letter, calls for a hybrid. "*I love . . . all who know the truth because of the truth, which lives in us and will be with us forever. Grace, mercy and peace from God the Father and from Jesus Christ, the Father's Son, will be with us in truth and love*" (verses 1–3).

Truth and love. Love and truth. Never one without the other. To pursue both is the Christian's singular task.

AUTHOR AND DATE

The author of this letter refers to himself simply as the "elder" (verse 1). Some believe this refers to an obscure figure known as "John the Elder," who is mentioned in fragments from Papias as also residing in the city of Ephesus. However, given the author of 1 John states he was eyewitness to the events of Jesus' life (see 1 John 1:1–3), and the internal evidence shows 2 and 3 John were written by that same author, the consensus of the early church was that John the disciple was the author of all three letters. Given the content in 2 John is largely dependent on 1 John, it is likely the author composed it shortly after penning the first letter, c. AD 90.

SITUATION

Unlike 1 John, in which the author makes no mention of his name or his intended audience, the letters of 2 and 3 John follow the standard conventions for ancient letters, listing a recipient and following a common formula for the introduction and conclusion. In this case, the recipient is known only as "the lady chosen by God" (verse 1). This "lady" may refer to an individual or to the congregation as a whole. John's purpose is again to combat false teaching in the church—in particular, that Jesus was divine but only *appeared* to be human.

KEY THEMES

- Love is an ultimate force, the essence of God and His command to us.
- The truth of Jesus Christ is the foundation of the gospel.
- Those who do not teach the truth do serious harm and should be treated seriously.

KEY VERSE

Anyone who runs ahead and does not continue in the teaching of Christ does not have God; whoever continues in the teaching has both the Father and the Son (verse 9).

CONTENTS

3 JOHN

John's third letter is to a man named Gaius. Whoever Gaius was, he has a special place in John's heart. John is writing to thank him for his hospitality.

In the early church, Christians would show hospitality to traveling prophets, teachers, and evangelists. Word was out that Gaius was exemplary in providing this kind of hospitality. He kept his door open and pantry stocked, and John is writing to commend him.

John's words are not so kind, however, for another man in the community named Diotrephes. Apparently, he was the opposite of Gaius. Where Gaius was accepting, Diotrephes was demanding. As John says, "Diotrephes, who loves to be first, will not welcome us. . . . Not satisfied with that, he even refuses to welcome other believers" (verses 9–10).

In a way, reading John's letters are like reading postcards that weren't intended for you. But in another sense, it's like getting personal letters from John.

By the way . . . are you more like Gaius or more like Diotrephes? Or, stated differently, do you love people or love the limelight?

If John were writing a note to you, what would he say?

AUTHOR AND DATE

Similar to 2 John, the author of this letter again identifies himself only as the "elder" (verse 1). Many of the early church fathers—including Cyril of Jerusalem, Jerome, and Augustine—accepted this letter (along with 1 and 2 John) as being authentic and written by the disciple John. While it is likely that 3 John was written after 1 John, c. AD 90, it is unknown whether the discipled penned it before, simultaneously, or after 2 John. It is quite probable that 2 and 3 John, along with Revelation, were the last of all the New Testament literature to be written.

SITUATION

The recipient of this letter, as noted above, is Gaius. While it is not possible to conclusively identify this individual, it is interesting to note the apostle Paul also refers to a "Gaius . . . whose *hospitality* I and the whole church here enjoy" (Romans 16:23, emphasis added). If this is the same person, Gaius was a Corinthian believer who showed hospitality to strangers and accompanied Paul on his third missionary journey. John's purpose is commend those (like Gaius) who practice hospitality and condemn those (like Diotrephes) who refuse to do so.

KEY THEMES

- When we help ministers of the gospel we become part of their ministry.
- We need to be generous toward one another.
- Personal pride has no place in ministry.

KEY VERSE

Dear friend, do not imitate what is evil but what is good. Anyone who does what is good is from God. Anyone who does what is evil has not seen God (verse 11).

CONTENTS

JUDE

A redwood tree fell in a California forest. Four hundred years old.

It wasn't destroyed by lightning. Storms had come and gone, but the tree stood. It wasn't felled by winds. Bent by their force, but never uprooted. The tree didn't fall to fire. It had stood when others collapsed.

What destroyed the redwood?

Insects. Termites devoured it from within. It had stood for four centuries against the elements from without but collapsed because of an attack within.

Jude warns that the same thing can happen to the church.

He wanted to write "about the salvation we share" (verse 3).

But he felt compelled to address a more somber issue—the danger of false teachers.

Apparently, some had entered the church. They were not students of the Word but, rather, promoters of sexual sin. They used God's grace as a license for passion. The only solution? "Contend for the faith that was once for all entrusted to God's holy people" (verse 3).

Jude is urgent in his warning. What destroyed the redwood tree can destroy a church. But he is equally urgent in his encouragement. "To Him who is able to keep you from stumbling, and to present you faultless before the presence of His glory with exceeding joy, to God our Savior" (verses 24–25 NKJV).

Can God really keep you from falling? To answer that, go to another tree on a barren hill. A tree older than time. A tree that covers the mistakes of your past and the problems of your future. Be assured—that tree will never fall.

AUTHOR AND DATE

The author of this letter refers to himself as "Jude, a bondservant of Jesus Christ, and brother of James" (verse 1). While several individuals named James appear in the New Testament, Clement of Alexandria, writing in the second century, stated the individual to which the author is referring was James the half-brother of Jesus, who was a leader in the early Jerusalem church. Other early church fathers such as Origen, Athanasius, Jerome, and Augustine made the same claim. Matthew states the names of Jesus' brothers were "James, Joseph, Simon and Judas" (13:55)—with "Jude" being a contracted form of the name "Judas"—and it is clear the author was well-known, respected, and active in the early church. Given the similarities between Jude and 2 Peter, it is likely the two were written around the same time, c. AD 67.

SITUATION

Given the examples the author cites from the Old Testament, it is likely he was writing to a group of Jewish Christians (similar to the recipients of the epistle of James). Jude states his original intent was to write about "the salvation we share," but he felt compelled to instead urge the believers "to contend for the faith that was once for all entrusted to God's holy people" (verse 3). He has evidently become aware of certain false teachers who have infiltrated the church, just as "the apostles of our Lord Jesus" predicted they would (verse 17). This group rejects spiritual authority, uses the doctrine of grace as a license to follow their own desires, and are self-indulgent "shepherds who feed only themselves" (verse 12). Jude wants to expose these false teachers for what they are and remind his readers of the true gospel they received.

KEY THEMES

- Each Christian should feel a responsibility to defend the truth.
- Stand against false teachers when you recognize them.
- Trust God to give you the strength and awareness to represent Him in the world.

KEY VERSE

To him who is able to keep you from stumbling and to present you before his glorious presence without fault and with great joy (verse 24).

CONTENTS

LESSON ONE

FELLOWSHIP WITH GOD

If we walk in the light as He is in the light, we have fellowship with one another, and the blood of Jesus Christ His Son cleanses us from all sin.
1 JOHN 1:7 NKJV

REFLECTION

People talk about *knowing* this or *believing* that or being *convinced* of something else. What is required for you to be one-hundred-percent sure about something? For example, how sure are you that Jesus really lived, that he claimed to be God, and that he is God in the flesh? Explain.

SITUATION

As one of Jesus' closest friends and most faithful followers, the apostle John was able to speak with authority about the reality and life-changing power of Christ's gospel message. In this first portion of his letter, he begins by reminding his readers he was an eyewitness to the events of Jesus' life. John then sets up a main theme to which he will return throughout his letter: God is light, and believers are to walk in that light. Even if we sin, we can still have a relationship with God if we confess our sin and accept the atoning sacrifice that Jesus made for us on the cross.

OBSERVATION

*Read 1 John 1:1–2:2 from the New International
Version or the New King James Version.*

NEW INTERNATIONAL VERSION

1:1 That which was from the beginning, which we have heard, which we have seen with our eyes, which we have looked at and our hands have touched—this we proclaim concerning the Word of life. 2 The life appeared; we have seen it and testify to it, and we proclaim to you the eternal life, which was with the Father and has appeared to us. 3 We proclaim to you what we have seen and heard, so that you also may have fellowship with us. And our fellowship is with the Father and with his Son, Jesus Christ. 4 We write this to make our joy complete.

5 This is the message we have heard from him and declare to you: God is light; in him there is no darkness at all. 6 If we claim to have fellowship with him and yet walk in the darkness, we lie and do not live out the truth. 7 But if we walk in the light, as he is in the light, we have fellowship with one another, and the blood of Jesus, his Son, purifies us from all sin.

8 If we claim to be without sin, we deceive ourselves and the truth is not in us. 9 If we confess our sins, he is faithful and just and will forgive us our sins and purify us from all unrighteousness. 10 If we claim we have not sinned, we make him out to be a liar and his word is not in us.

2:1 My dear children, I write this to you so that you will not sin. But if anybody does sin, we have an advocate with the Father—Jesus Christ, the Righteous One. 2 He is the atoning sacrifice for our sins, and not only for ours but also for the sins of the whole world.

NEW KING JAMES VERSION

1:1 That which was from the beginning, which we have heard, which we have seen with our eyes, which we have looked upon, and our hands have handled, concerning the Word of life— 2 the life was manifested, and we have seen, and bear witness, and declare to you that eternal life which was with the Father and was manifested to us— ³ that which we have seen and heard we declare to you, that you also may have fellowship with us; and truly our fellowship is with the Father and with His Son Jesus Christ. ⁴ And these things we write to you that your joy may be full.

⁵ This is the message which we have heard from Him and declare to you, that God is light and in Him is no darkness at all. ⁶ If we say that we have fellowship with Him, and walk in darkness, we lie and do not practice the truth. ⁷ But if we walk in the light as He is in the light, we have fellowship with one another, and the blood of Jesus Christ His Son cleanses us from all sin.

⁸ If we say that we have no sin, we deceive ourselves, and the truth is not in us. ⁹ If we confess our sins, He is faithful and just to forgive us our sins and to cleanse us from all unrighteousness. ¹⁰ If we say that we have not sinned, we make Him a liar, and His word is not in us.

²:¹ My little children, these things I write to you, so that you may not sin. And if anyone sins, we have an Advocate with the Father, Jesus Christ the righteous. ² And He Himself is the propitiation for our sins, and not for ours only but also for the whole world.

EXPLORATION

1. How does John establish his authority to write about Christ and his gospel message?

_____

_____

_____

_____

_____

_____

_____

_____

2. Why does it matter that John heard and saw and touched Jesus?

3. What does John mean by the term *fellowship*?

4. How would you explain the symbolism of *light* and *darkness* in this passage?

5. What does John say about those who claim to be without sin?

6. What help and resources do believers in Christ have when they sin?

INSPIRATION

"For God so loved the world that he gave his one and only Son, that whoever believes in him shall not perish but have eternal life" (John 3:16).

The word *whoever* in this verse from the disciple John unfurls it as a banner for the ages. *Whoever* unrolls the welcome mat of heaven to humanity. *Whoever* invites the world to God.

Jesus could have so easily narrowed the scope, changing *whoever* into *whatever*. "Whatever Jew believes" or "whatever woman follows me." But he used no qualifier. The pronoun is wonderfully indefinite. After all, who isn't a *whoever*?

The word sledgehammers racial fences and dynamites social classes. It bypasses gender borders and surpasses ancient traditions. *Whoever* makes it clear: God exports his grace worldwide. For those who attempt to restrict it, Jesus has a word: *whoever*. . . .

The apostle Paul assures us that "the grace of God has appeared . . . to all people" (Titus 2:11). He contends that Jesus Christ sacrificed himself "as a ransom for all people" (1 Timothy 2:6). Peter affirms that God "is patient . . . not wanting anyone to perish, but everyone to come to repentance (2 Peter 3:9). God's gospel has a *whoever* policy. . . .

We lose much in life—sobriety, solvency, and sanity. We lose jobs and chances, and we lose at love. We lose youth and its vigor, idealism and its dreams. We lose much, but we never lose our place on God's "whoever" list. *Whoever*—God's wonderful word of welcome.

I love to hear my wife say "whoever." Sometimes I detect my favorite fragrance wafting from the kitchen: strawberry cake. I follow the smell like a bird dog follows a trail until I'm standing over the just-baked, just-iced pan of pure pleasure. Yet I've learned to still my fork until Denalyn gives clearance.

"Who is it for?" I ask.

She might break my heart. "It's for a birthday party, Max. Don't touch it!" Or, "For a friend. Stay away."

Or she might throw open the door of delight. "Whoever."

And since I qualify as a "whoever," I say "yes."

I so hope you will too. Not to the cake, but to God. No status too low. No hour too late. No place too far. However. Whenever. Wherever.

Whoever includes you . . . forever. (From *3:16: The Numbers of Hope* by Max Lucado.)

REACTION

7. What promise does the Bible give that you can have fellowship with God?

---

8. How do you react to the idea God has a "whoever" policy when it comes to salvation?

---

9. What is required on your part to take advantage of God's "whoever" policy?

---

10. Why is it important that Jesus actually lived as a human being on this earth?

---

11. What does the fact Jesus came into this world as a human tell you about God's desire to have fellowship with you?

12. How would you explain *eternal life* to a person who did not grow up in church?

LIFE LESSONS

Fellowship. It's a word that gets tossed around a lot in Christian circles. For many it's just a euphemism for cookies and punch in the church basement. But the biblical term means so much more. True fellowship (or community) means *that which is shared in common.* The moment we trust in Christ to forgive our sins and make us right with God, we come alive spiritually and the very life of the Almighty flows in and through us. We become God's children—brothers and sisters in an eternal family. We share an eternal connection with God and with one another, a profound oneness, and an exciting partnership in the gospel.

DEVOTION

Lord Jesus, thank you for leaving heaven and "moving into earth's neighborhood." Thank you that you came to this earth and gave your life so that we might have fellowship with God. Thank you even more for providing a way for me to share in the endless blessings of eternal life.

JOURNALING

What are some practical things you can do to strengthen you fellowship with other believers?

FOR FURTHER READING

To complete the books of 1, 2, 3 John and Jude during this twelve-part study, read 1 John 1:1–2:2. For more Bible passages about fellowship, read Ecclesiastes 4:9–12; Luke 24:13–16; Acts 2:42–47; Romans 1:11–12; Philippians 1:3–5, 1 Thessalonians 5:4–11; and Hebrews 10:24–25.

OBEDIENCE TO GOD

We know that we have come to know
[Christ] if we keep his commands.
1 JOHN 2:3

11

REFLECTION

People have many ways of trying to gauge the genuineness of a person's faith: how much one gives, or how often the person attends church, or how well he or she can discuss theology and the Bible. What are some of the traits you notice in a person that suggest he or she has made an authentic commitment to Christ? Why those particular characteristics?

SITUATION

In this next section of John's letter, he reminds his readers that believers in Christ can enjoy an ever-deepening fellowship with God by leading a life marked by obedience, love, and holiness. In fact, obedience to Christ's commands is the hallmark of a believer's life—especially as it relates to following Jesus' greatest commandments to "love the Lord your God . . . and love your neighbor as yourself" (Matthew 22:37, 39). Love for the *world*, on the other hand, reveals a person does not know Christ and that "love for the Father is not in them" (1 John 2:15).

OBSERVATION

*Read 1 John 2:3–17 from the New International
Version or the New King James Version.*

NEW INTERNATIONAL VERSION

[3] We know that we have come to know him if we keep his commands.
[4] Whoever says, "I know him," but does not do what he commands is a
liar, and the truth is not in that person. [5] But if anyone obeys his word,
love for God is truly made complete in them. This is how we know we are
in him: [6] Whoever claims to live in him must live as Jesus did.

[7] Dear friends, I am not writing you a new command but an old one,
which you have had since the beginning. This old command is the message you have heard. [8] Yet I am writing you a new command; its truth is
seen in him and in you, because the darkness is passing and the true light
is already shining.

[9] Anyone who claims to be in the light but hates a brother or sister
is still in the darkness. [10] Anyone who loves their brother and sister lives
in the light, and there is nothing in them to make them stumble. [11] But
anyone who hates a brother or sister is in the darkness and walks around
in the darkness. They do not know where they are going, because the
darkness has blinded them.

[12] I am writing to you, dear children,
> because your sins have been forgiven on account of his name.

[13] I am writing to you, fathers,
> because you know him who is from the beginning.

I am writing to you, young men,
> because you have overcome the evil one.

[14] I write to you, dear children,
> because you know the Father.

I write to you, fathers,
> because you know him who is from the beginning.

> I write to you, young men,
>> because you are strong,
>> and the word of God lives in you,
>> and you have overcome the evil one.

[15] Do not love the world or anything in the world. If anyone loves the world, love for the Father is not in them. [16] For everything in the world—the lust of the flesh, the lust of the eyes, and the pride of life—comes not from the Father but from the world. [17] The world and its desires pass away, but whoever does the will of God lives forever.

NEW KING JAMES VERSION

[3] Now by this we know that we know Him, if we keep His commandments. [4] He who says, "I know Him," and does not keep His commandments, is a liar, and the truth is not in him. [5] But whoever keeps His word, truly the love of God is perfected in him. By this we know that we are in Him. [6] He who says he abides in Him ought himself also to walk just as He walked.

[7] Brethren, I write no new commandment to you, but an old commandment which you have had from the beginning. The old commandment is the word which you heard from the beginning. [8] Again, a new commandment I write to you, which thing is true in Him and in you, because the darkness is passing away, and the true light is already shining.

[9] He who says he is in the light, and hates his brother, is in darkness until now. [10] He who loves his brother abides in the light, and there is no cause for stumbling in him. [11] But he who hates his brother is in darkness and walks in darkness, and does not know where he is going, because the darkness has blinded his eyes.

> [12] I write to you, little children,
> Because your sins are forgiven you for His name's sake.
> [13] I write to you, fathers,
> Because you have known Him who is from the beginning.

I write to you, young men,

Because you have overcome the wicked one.

I write to you, little children,

Because you have known the Father.

¹⁴ I have written to you, fathers,

Because you have known Him who is from the beginning.

I have written to you, young men,

Because you are strong, and the word of God abides in you,

And you have overcome the wicked one.

¹⁵ Do not love the world or the things in the world. If anyone loves the world, the love of the Father is not in him. ¹⁶ For all that is in the world—the lust of the flesh, the lust of the eyes, and the pride of life—is not of the Father but is of the world. ¹⁷ And the world is passing away, and the lust of it; but he who does the will of God abides forever.

EXPLORATION

1. John writes that no one can obey God perfectly (see 1:8 and 2:4). Given this, how can you be sure your faith is genuine?

2. What does John say is the evidence that a person is truly following Christ?

3. What does it mean, in practical terms, to "live as Jesus did" (verse 6)?

4. Given John's message in verses 9–11, how would you help a fellow Christian who held bitterness and resentment against another person?

5. Which of the promises in verses 12–14 are most encouraging to you personally? Why?

6. How can you know when you are guilty of loving the world?

INSPIRATION

It took three hundred years, but the Black Plague finally reached the quaint village of Eyam, England. George Viccars, a tailor, unpacked a parcel shipped from London. The cloth he'd ordered had arrived. But as he opened and shook it, he released plague-infected fleas. Within four days he was dead, and the village was doomed.

The town unselfishly quarantined itself, seeking to protect the region. Other villages deposited food in an open field and left the people of Eyam to die alone. But to everyone's amazement, many survived. A year later, when outsiders again visited the town, they found half the residents had resisted the disease. How so? They had touched it. Breathed it. One surviving mother had buried six children and her husband in one week. The gravedigger had handled hundreds of diseased corpses yet hadn't died. Why not? How did they survive?

Lineage. Through DNA studies of descendants, scientists found proof of a disease-blocking gene. The gene garrisoned the white blood cells, preventing the bacteria from gaining entrance. The plague, in other words, could touch people with this gene but not kill them. Hence a sub-populace swam in a sea of infection but emerged untouched. All because they had the right parents. What's the secret for surviving the Black Plague? Pick the right ancestry.

Of course, they couldn't. But by God, you can. You can select your spiritual father. You can change your family tree from that of Adam to God. And when you do, he moves in. His resistance becomes your resistance. His Teflon coating becomes yours. Sin may entice you, but will never enslave you. Sin may, and will, touch you, discourage you, and distract you, but it cannot condemn you. Christ is in you, and you are in him, and "there is no condemnation for those who belong to Christ Jesus" (Romans 8:1).

Can I urge you to trust this truth? Let your constant prayer be this: "Lord, I receive your work. My sins are pardoned." Trust the work of God *for* you. Then trust the presence of Christ *in* you. Take frequent, refreshing drinks from his well of grace. You need regular reminders that you are not fatally afflicted! Don't live as though you are. (From *Come Thirsty* by Max Lucado.)

REACTION

7. The secret as to how the Eyam villagers were able to survive death from the Black Plague was *lineage*. How is the same true of believers in Christ when it comes to the effects of sin?

_____

_____

_____

8. What are some ways you can remind yourself today that you are not "fatally afflicted" if you have confessed your sins to God?

_____

_____

_____

9. How does the truth of "Christ in you" encourage you as you seek to live a life of obedience?

_____

_____

_____

10. What are some ways God's light has grown brighter in you in recent months?

_____

_____

_____

11. What are some attitudes you have that you would consider "worldly"?

---

12. How are you seeking to change those attitudes? What progress are you making?

LIFE LESSONS

We have to be careful how we interpret John's words. If obedient living and love are the only "proof" our faith is real, what happens when we speak ill of a coworker or act selfishly toward a family member? Does our sin reveal we weren't true believers but only "make-believers"? Does our failure mean we lose our salvation? No and no. Fellowship with God is both a fact and a process. Because of our faith in Christ's perfect work, we have fellowship with God. But we also *grow* in our knowledge of him. We are *transformed* over time. Nobody obeys all the time. Every Christian is guilty of failing to love. But God's grace is greater than all our sins, and when we humbly acknowledge our wrongs, we find fresh forgiveness and restoration to fellowship.

DEVOTION

Lord, continue to change our hearts. Give us an ever-deepening desire to live in the way you intend for us to live—the way that brings you glory. Help us to walk in your light and put aside the things of the world. Direct us to seek your will and follow your commands.

JOURNALING

In what ways is *darkness* a good metaphor for a life of disobedience?

_____

_____

_____

_____

_____

_____

_____

_____

_____

_____

_____

_____

_____

_____

_____

_____

_____

_____

FOR FURTHER READING

To complete the books of 1, 2, 3 John and Jude during this twelve-part study, read 1 John 2:3–17. For more Bible passages on obedience, read Exodus 19:3–6; Deuteronomy 4:30–32; 5:28–29; 28:1–2; 1 Samuel 15:22–23; John 14:21, 30–31; 15:10; Romans 5:19; and James 1:25.

ENEMIES OF CHRIST!

*Who is a liar but he who denies that Jesus
is the Christ? . . . Whoever denies the Son
does not have the Father either; he who
acknowledges the Son has the Father also.*

1 JOHN 2:22–23 NKJV

21

REFLECTION

We live in an age in which tolerance is viewed as one of the highest virtues and it is considered wrong to ever call into question the beliefs of another person. When do you think tolerance is right and called for? When is it foolish—and even dangerous—to be tolerant of certain beliefs?

SITUATION

John has now established what it looks like for people to have a relationship with Christ and truly know him as their Lord and Savior. With this in mind, he now addresses the central issue at hand: exposing false teachers in the church who have no love for God and are leading the believers astray. John reminds his readers that they are living in the "last hour" (verse 18) and have been warned that at such a time these false teachers will arise. Even in the early days of Christianity, it is apparent that wherever people proclaimed God's truth, the enemy promptly counterattacked by inspiring smooth-talking preachers to spout an alternate gospel. John challenges his readers to identify these individuals and regard them as enemies of Christ.

OBSERVATION

*Read 1 John 2:18–29 from the New International
Version or the New King James Version.*

NEW INTERNATIONAL VERSION

[18] Dear children, this is the last hour; and as you have heard that the antichrist is coming, even now many antichrists have come. This is how we know it is the last hour. [19] They went out from us, but they did not really belong to us. For if they had belonged to us, they would have remained with us; but their going showed that none of them belonged to us.

[20] But you have an anointing from the Holy One, and all of you know the truth. [21] I do not write to you because you do not know the truth, but because you do know it and because no lie comes from the truth. [22] Who is the liar? It is whoever denies that Jesus is the Christ. Such a person is the antichrist—denying the Father and the Son. [23] No one who denies the Son has the Father; whoever acknowledges the Son has the Father also.

[24] As for you, see that what you have heard from the beginning remains in you. If it does, you also will remain in the Son and in the Father. [25] And this is what he promised us—eternal life.

[26] I am writing these things to you about those who are trying to lead you astray. [27] As for you, the anointing you received from him remains in you, and you do not need anyone to teach you. But as his anointing teaches you about all things and as that anointing is real, not counterfeit—just as it has taught you, remain in him.

[28] And now, dear children, continue in him, so that when he appears we may be confident and unashamed before him at his coming.

[29] If you know that he is righteous, you know that everyone who does what is right has been born of him.

NEW KING JAMES VERSION

[18] Little children, it is the last hour; and as you have heard that the Antichrist is coming, even now many antichrists have come, by which

we know that it is the last hour. [19] They went out from us, but they were not of us; for if they had been of us, they would have continued with us; but they went out that they might be made manifest, that none of them were of us.

[20] But you have an anointing from the Holy One, and you know all things. [21] I have not written to you because you do not know the truth, but because you know it, and that no lie is of the truth.

[22] Who is a liar but he who denies that Jesus is the Christ? He is antichrist who denies the Father and the Son. [23] Whoever denies the Son does not have the Father either; he who acknowledges the Son has the Father also.

[24] Therefore let that abide in you which you heard from the beginning. If what you heard from the beginning abides in you, you also will abide in the Son and in the Father. [25] And this is the promise that He has promised us—eternal life.

[26] These things I have written to you concerning those who try to deceive you. [27] But the anointing which you have received from Him abides in you, and you do not need that anyone teach you; but as the same anointing teaches you concerning all things, and is true, and is not a lie, and just as it has taught you, you will abide in Him.

[28] And now, little children, abide in Him, that when He appears, we may have confidence and not be ashamed before Him at His coming. [29] If you know that He is righteous, you know that everyone who practices righteousness is born of Him.

EXPLORATION

1. What evidence does John provide that believers are living in "the last hour" (verse 18)?

2. What is the connection and/or difference between the "Antichrist" (singular) and "antichrists" (plural) in verse 18 (NKJV)?

3. According to John, what constitutes being an *enemy* of Christ?

4. What resources does John say God gave you to keep you from being led astray?

5. What is the message for those who say they love God but can't accept that Jesus is anything more than a good man and great teacher?

6. Read John 15:4–8. What is the importance of abiding in Christ?

INSPIRATION

You've seen them. The talk is smooth. The vocabulary eloquent. The appearance genuine. They are on your television. They are on your radio. They may even be in your pulpit.

May I speak candidly?

The time has come to tolerate religious hucksters no longer. These seekers of "sanctimoney" have stained the reputation of Christianity. They have muddied the altars and shattered the stained glass. They manipulate the easily deceived. They are not governed by God; they are governed by greed. They are not led by the Spirit; they are propelled by pride. They are marshmallow phonies who excel in emotion and fail in doctrine. They strip-mine faith to get a dollar and rape the pew to get a payment.

Our master unveiled their scams and so must we. How? By recognizing them. Two trademarks give them away. One, they emphasize their profit more than the Prophet.

In the church in Crete some people made a living off the gullible souls in the church. Paul had strong words about them. "They must be silenced, because they are disrupting whole households by teaching things they ought not to teach—and that for the sake of dishonest gain" (Titus 1:11).

Listen carefully to the television evangelists. Analyze the words of the radio preachers. Note the emphasis of the message. What is the burden? Your salvation or your donation? Monitor what is said. Is money always needed yesterday? Are you promised health if you give and hell if you don't? If so, ignore them.

A second characteristic of ecclesiastical con artists: they build more fences than they build faith. . . . They present themselves as pioneers that the mainline church couldn't stomach, but, in reality, they are lone wolves on the prowl. They have franchised an approach and want to protect it. Their bread and butter is the uniqueness of their faith. Only they can give you what you need. Their cure-all kit is the solution to your aches. . . .

Their aim is to cultivate a clientele of loyal checkbooks. "I urge you, brothers and sisters, to watch out for those who cause divisions and put obstacles in your way that are contrary to the teaching you have learned. Keep away from them. For such people are not serving our Lord Christ, but their own appetites. By smooth talk and flattery they deceive the minds of naive people" (Romans 16:17–18). (From *And the Angels Were Silent* by Max Lucado.)

REACTION

7. What are two key trademarks of religious hucksters? How can you identify them?

8. What are some examples you have seen of false teaching in the church today?

9. What instructions does Paul give in Titus 1:11 and Romans 16:17–18 for how to deal with "ecclesiastical con artists"?

10. How can you tell, as you are being guided by the Holy Spirit, that a teaching is of God?

_____

_____

_____

11. How can being in community and having fellowship with other believers help you when it comes to determining whether a teaching is true or false?

_____

_____

_____

12. What are some specific protective measures you need to take to better prepare for the false teachers you are likely to encounter?

_____

_____

_____

LIFE LESSONS

As warnings go, here's one from Paul that's a doozy: "Satan himself masquerades as an angel of light" (2 Corinthians 11:14). This is a sobering reminder that some things that seem right can actually be deadly! We have a sworn enemy who wrote the book on deception. He's an expert at blinding people to what's true, and he would like nothing more than to bring about our death (see John 8:44)! And yet, because we are God's children, indwelt by God's Spirit, we do not have to cower in fear. Our responsibility is to remain sober minded and alert, keep up our guard, and filter everything we hear through the grid of God's truth. We are to critically and carefully evaluate *all* the spiritual teachings and theological claims we hear.

DEVOTION

Heavenly Father, continue to guide us in your truth. Fill us, guard us, and shape us into the people you want us to be. Teach us how to think rightly and how to live in a manner that pleases you and brings glory to you. We yield our hearts and our minds—and our very lives—to you.

JOURNALING

Have you ever felt the need to leave a particular church? If so, what were your reasons?

FOR FURTHER READING

To complete the books of 1, 2, 3 John and Jude during this twelve-part study, read 1 John 2:18–29. For more Bible passages on spiritual deception, read Romans 16:18; 2 Corinthians 11:13; Galatians 1:8; Ephesians 4:14; 2 Thessalonians 2:1–4; 2 Timothy 3:13; Titus 1:10; and 2 John 1:7.

LESSON FOUR

CHIPS OFF THE OLD BLOCK

*See what great love the Father has lavished
on us, that we should be called children
of God! And that is what we are!*

1 JOHN 3:1

REFLECTION

We use some interesting expressions to refer to the ways children resemble their parents. "The apple didn't fall far from the tree." "She's the spitting image of her mom. "Like father, like son." In what ways are you like your mom and dad? In what ways are you different?

SITUATION

John has just noted the appearance of false teachers in the church is an indication that we are living in the "last days." This being the case, the hope we have of Jesus' return should naturally produce a desire within us to continually strive to live in a godly manner and pursue God's holiness. John reminds us that when believers exhibit the character of God in their behavior—following Jesus' example to the point of even laying down our lives for one another— the world will recognize us as God's children.

We are "chips off the old block," as the saying goes, and we can rest in the confidence that comes from knowing that God truly dwells within us.

OBSERVATION

Read 1 John 3:1–24 from the New International Version or the New King James Version.

NEW INTERNATIONAL VERSION

[1] See what great love the Father has lavished on us, that we should be called children of God! And that is what we are! The reason the world does not know us is that it did not know him. [2] Dear friends, now we are children of God, and what we will be has not yet been made known. But we know that when Christ appears, we shall be like him, for we shall see him as he is. [3] All who have this hope in him purify themselves, just as he is pure.

[4] Everyone who sins breaks the law; in fact, sin is lawlessness. [5] But you know that he appeared so that he might take away our sins. And in him is no sin. [6] No one who lives in him keeps on sinning. No one who continues to sin has either seen him or known him.

[7] Dear children, do not let anyone lead you astray. The one who does what is right is righteous, just as he is righteous. [8] The one who does what is sinful is of the devil, because the devil has been sinning from the beginning. The reason the Son of God appeared was to destroy the devil's work. [9] No one who is born of God will continue to sin, because God's seed remains in them; they cannot go on sinning, because they have been born of God. [10] This is how we know who the children of God are and who the children of the devil are: Anyone who does not do what is right is not God's child, nor is anyone who does not love their brother and sister.

[11] For this is the message you heard from the beginning: We should love one another. [12] Do not be like Cain, who belonged to the evil one and murdered his brother. And why did he murder him? Because his own

actions were evil and his brother's were righteous. [13] Do not be surprised, my brothers and sisters, if the world hates you. [14] We know that we have passed from death to life, because we love each other. Anyone who does not love remains in death. [15] Anyone who hates a brother or sister is a murderer, and you know that no murderer has eternal life residing in him.

[16] This is how we know what love is: Jesus Christ laid down his life for us. And we ought to lay down our lives for our brothers and sisters. [17] If anyone has material possessions and sees a brother or sister in need but has no pity on them, how can the love of God be in that person? [18] Dear children, let us not love with words or speech but with actions and in truth.

[19] This is how we know that we belong to the truth and how we set our hearts at rest in his presence: [20] If our hearts condemn us, we know that God is greater than our hearts, and he knows everything. [21] Dear friends, if our hearts do not condemn us, we have confidence before God [22] and receive from him anything we ask, because we keep his commands and do what pleases him. [23] And this is his command: to believe in the name of his Son, Jesus Christ, and to love one another as he commanded us. [24] The one who keeps God's commands lives in him, and he in them. And this is how we know that he lives in us: We know it by the Spirit he gave us.

NEW KING JAMES VERSION

[1] Behold what manner of love the Father has bestowed on us, that we should be called children of God! Therefore the world does not know us, because it did not know Him. [2] Beloved, now we are children of God; and it has not yet been revealed what we shall be, but we know that when He is revealed, we shall be like Him, for we shall see Him as He is. [3] And everyone who has this hope in Him purifies himself, just as He is pure.

[4] Whoever commits sin also commits lawlessness, and sin is lawlessness. [5] And you know that He was manifested to take away our sins, and in Him there is no sin. [6] Whoever abides in Him does not sin. Whoever sins has neither seen Him nor known Him.

⁷ Little children, let no one deceive you. He who practices righteousness is righteous, just as He is righteous. ⁸ He who sins is of the devil, for the devil has sinned from the beginning. For this purpose the Son of God was manifested, that He might destroy the works of the devil. ⁹ Whoever has been born of God does not sin, for His seed remains in him; and he cannot sin, because he has been born of God.

¹⁰ In this the children of God and the children of the devil are manifest: Whoever does not practice righteousness is not of God, nor is he who does not love his brother. ¹¹ For this is the message that you heard from the beginning, that we should love one another, ¹² not as Cain who was of the wicked one and murdered his brother. And why did he murder him? Because his works were evil and his brother's righteous.

¹³ Do not marvel, my brethren, if the world hates you. ¹⁴ We know that we have passed from death to life, because we love the brethren. He who does not love his brother abides in death. ¹⁵ Whoever hates his brother is a murderer, and you know that no murderer has eternal life abiding in him.

¹⁶ By this we know love, because He laid down His life for us. And we also ought to lay down our lives for the brethren. ¹⁷ But whoever has this world's goods, and sees his brother in need, and shuts up his heart from him, how does the love of God abide in him?

¹⁸ My little children, let us not love in word or in tongue, but in deed and in truth. ¹⁹ And by this we know that we are of the truth, and shall assure our hearts before Him. ²⁰ For if our heart condemns us, God is greater than our heart, and knows all things. ²¹ Beloved, if our heart does not condemn us, we have confidence toward God. ²² And whatever we ask we receive from Him, because we keep His commandments and do those things that are pleasing in His sight. ²³ And this is His commandment: that we should believe on the name of His Son Jesus Christ and love one another, as He gave us commandment.

²⁴ Now he who keeps His commandments abides in Him, and He in him. And by this we know that He abides in us, by the Spirit whom He has given us.

EXPLORATION

1. How does John say God lavished his love on believers in Christ?

2. What are some advantages of being a child of God?

3. What does John say your life should look like if you are abiding in Christ?

4. John indicates that not everyone is a child of God (see verse 10). Do you think most people agree with this idea? Why or why not?

5. What is "the devil's work" (verse 8). How has Christ destroyed it?

6. Why should you not be surprised "if the world hates you" (verse 13)?

_____

_____

_____

_____

INSPIRATION

God not only forgives you but he also adopts you. Through a dramatic series of events, you go from condemned orphan with no hope to an adopted child with no fear.

Here is how it happens. You come before the judgment seat of God full of rebellion and mistakes. Because of his justice he cannot dismiss your sin, but because of his love he cannot dismiss you. So, in an act which stunned the heavens, he punished himself on the cross for your sins. God's justice and love are equally honored. And you, God's creation, are forgiven. But the story doesn't end with God's forgiveness.

"For you did not receive the spirit of bondage again to fear, but you received the Spirit of adoption by whom we cry out, 'Abba, Father.' The Spirit Himself bears witness with our spirit that we are children of God" (Romans 8:15–16 NKJV). . . .

It would be enough if God just cleansed your name, but he does more. He gives you _his_ name. It would be enough if God just set you free, but he does more. He takes you home. He takes you home to the Great House of God.

Adoptive parents understand this more than anyone. I certainly don't mean to offend any biological parents—I'm one myself. We biological parents know well the earnest longing to have a child. But in many cases our cribs were filled easily. We decided to have a child and a child came. In fact, sometimes the child came with no decision. I've heard of unplanned pregnancies, but I've never heard of an unplanned adoption.

That's why adoptive parents understand God's passion to adopt us. They know what it means to feel an empty space inside. They know what it means to hunt, to set out on a mission, and take responsibility for a child with a spotted past and a dubious future. If anybody understands God's ardor for his children, it's someone who has rescued an orphan from despair, for that is what God has done for us.

God has adopted you. God sought you, found you, signed the papers and took you home. (From *The Great House of God* by Max Lucado.)

REACTION

7. How do you react when you ponder the reality of "divine adoption"?

_____

_____

_____

_____

8. The reality is that Christians sin daily. How do we reconcile this with the statements that God's children "cannot go on sinning" (verse 9)?

_____

_____

_____

_____

9. Assuming you have put your faith in Christ, what are some ways (small or large) you have begun to resemble your Father in heaven?

_____

_____

_____

_____

10. If Christ came back today, would you be more excited or more ashamed? Why?

11. What does it mean that you have "been born of God" (verse 9)?

12. What specific actions will you take today so that—by the Spirit's grace and help—you more closely resemble your heavenly Father?

LIFE LESSONS

Someone once observed that Christians do not make it their goal not to sin—they make it their goal not to sin *too much*. Such a mindset completely misses the truth about holiness. Who would knowingly drink a glass of water containing "just a few drops" of toxic chemicals? Nobody! You would as soon guzzle a full bottle of deadly poison! So why do we tolerate "little" sins? As the children of a holy God, we are called to reflect his character and represent him to the world. It is a serious challenge and a sobering responsibility. But it is not impossible. God has given us his truth, his Spirit, and his people (the church) to enable us to live as he wants.

DEVOTION

Father, you loved us so much that you sought us, forgave us, and adopted us into your family. We really are your children! Thank you for your grace. Today, we ask that you would continue to shape us into the likeness of Christ and complete the good work you have begun in us.

JOURNALING

What does it really mean for you to love your brothers and sisters in Christ?

FOR FURTHER READING

To complete the books of 1, 2, 3 John and Jude during this twelve-part study, read 1 John 3:1–24. For more Bible passages on divine sonship, read Deuteronomy 14:2; Isaiah 63:16; Romans 8:15; 2 Corinthians 6:18; Galatians 3:26; 4:5–6; Ephesians 2:19; 3:15; and Hebrews 2:11.

SPIRITUAL DISCERNMENT

Beloved, do not believe every spirit, but test the spirits, whether they are of God; because many false prophets have gone out into the world.

1 JOHN 4:1 NKJV

REFLECTION

Our world is one noisy place. Every moment of every day, advertisers, marketers, politicians, and pundits are vying to get our attention, influence our opinions, and alter our behavior. What criteria do you use to judge whether a commercial, candidate, cause, or a claim is legitimate?

SITUATION

John has noted that the Spirit of God, who dwells within true followers of Christ, testifies to the fact we are the beloved children of God. Yet the Holy Spirit also helps us to discern those who are *not* walking in God's light . . . those who are attempting to lead us astray with smooth-sounding (but false) words. John challenges us to *test* everything we hear against the truth we find in God's Word and rely on the guidance of the Holy Spirit for direction. As we do this, we will begin to discern the enemy's deceptions and not allow them to take root in our lives.

OBSERVATION

*Read 1 John 4:1–6 from the New International
Version or the New King James Version.*

NEW INTERNATIONAL VERSION

[1] Dear friends, do not believe every spirit, but test the spirits to see whether they are from God, because many false prophets have gone out into the world. [2] This is how you can recognize the Spirit of God: Every spirit that acknowledges that Jesus Christ has come in the flesh is from God, [3] but every spirit that does not acknowledge Jesus is not from God. This is the spirit of the antichrist, which you have heard is coming and even now is already in the world.

[4] You, dear children, are from God and have overcome them, because the one who is in you is greater than the one who is in the world. [5] They are from the world and therefore speak from the viewpoint of the world, and the world listens to them. [6] We are from God, and whoever knows God listens to us; but whoever is not from God does not listen to us. This is how we recognize the Spirit of truth and the spirit of falsehood.

NEW KING JAMES VERSION

[1] Beloved, do not believe every spirit, but test the spirits, whether they are of God; because many false prophets have gone out into the world. [2] By this you know the Spirit of God: Every spirit that confesses that Jesus Christ has come in the flesh is of God, [3] and every spirit that does not confess that Jesus Christ has come in the flesh is not of God. And this is the spirit of the Antichrist, which you have heard was coming, and is now already in the world.

[4] You are of God, little children, and have overcome them, because He who is in you is greater than he who is in the world. [5] They are of the world. Therefore they speak as of the world, and the world hears them. [6] We are of God. He who knows God hears us; he who is not of God does not hear us. By this we know the spirit of truth and the spirit of error.

EXPLORATION

1. What do you think it means to "test the spirits" (verse 1)?

2. What are the standards given by John for determining the validity of spiritual claims?

3. How can believers in Christ know they will overcome any spirits that come against them?

4. Why is it so important to be indwelt by the Holy Spirit?

5. John writes that "whoever knows God listens to us" (verse 6). How does knowing what the Bible says help you to discern what is and what isn't from God?

_____

_____

_____

_____

_____

_____

6. What are some ways you are actively seeking to listen to God's truth?

_____

_____

_____

_____

_____

_____

INSPIRATION

Many years ago, I watched the television adaptation of the drama *The Miracle Worker*, the compelling story of two females with great resolve: Helen Keller and Anne Sullivan. Helen was born in 1880. She wasn't yet two when she contracted an illness that left her blind, deaf, and mute. When Helen was seven years old, Annie, a young, partially blind teacher, came to the Kellers' Alabama home to serve as Helen's teacher.

Helen's brother James tried to convince Annie to quit. The teacher wouldn't consider it. She was resolved to help Helen function in a world of sight and sound. Helen was as stubborn as her teacher. Locked in a frightening, lonely world, she misinterpreted Annie's attempts. The result was a battle of wills. Over and over Annie pressed sign language into Helen's palm. Helen pulled back. Annie persisted. Helen resisted.

Finally, in a moment of high drama, a breakthrough. During a fevered exchange near the water pump, Annie placed one of Helen's hands under the spout of flowing water. Into the other hand she spelled out w-a-t-e-r. Over and over, w-a-t-e-r. Helen pulled back. Annie kept signing. W-a-t-e-r.

All of a sudden Helen stopped. She placed her hand on her teacher's and repeated the letters w-a-t-e-r. Annie beamed. She lifted Helen's hand onto her own cheek and nodded vigorously. "Yes, yes, yes! W-a-t-e-r." Helen spelled it again: w-a-t-e-r. Helen pulled Annie around the yard, spelling out the words. G-r-o-u-n-d. P-o-r-c-h. P-u-m-p. It was a victory parade.

Jesus' arrival on our earth celebrates a similar moment for us—God breaking through to our world. In a feeding stall of all places. He will not leave us in the dark. He is the pursuer, the teacher. He won't sit back while we miss out. So he entered our world. He sends signals and messages: H-o-p-e. L-i-f-e. He cracks the shell of our world and invites us to peek into his. And every so often a seeking soul looks up.

May you be one of them.

When God sends signs, be faithful. Let them lead you to Scripture.

As Scripture directs, be humble. Let it lead you to worship.

And as you worship the Son, be grateful. He will lead you home. (From *Because of Bethlehem* by Max Lucado.)

REACTION

7. How was Anne Sullivan able to breakthrough into Hellen Keller's world? How is this similar to the way God breaks through with understanding into our lives?

----

8. What are some of the "signals and messages" that Jesus sends to our world?

9. What are some things you are doing to be better attuned to the messages God is sending?

10. When John says to "test the spirits," he means to test the spirit behind various ideas. What popular contemporary teachings do you regard as dangerous? Why?

11. Which do you think wields the greatest influence in our culture, in terms of shaping public opinion: the educational system, the entertainment industry, or the church? Why?

_____

_____

_____

_____

_____

12. What are some areas in your life right now when you need greater spiritual discernment?

_____

_____

_____

_____

LIFE LESSONS

In so many words, the apostle Paul observed we all have to choose our own "craziness" . . . we can either embrace the "foolishness" of the gospel (see 1 Corinthians 1:18) or we can decide to live by the nonsensical values of this world (see 1 Corinthians 3:19). What about you? By what belief system are you ordering your life? Do you pay more attention to the clamor and contradictory messages of culture? Or do you make it your moment-by-moment goal to hear and follow the quiet counsel of Christ? Ask God to help you learn the discipline of "testing the spirits." Few abilities are as crucial as knowing how to discern what is true and what is not.

DEVOTION

Holy Spirit of God, thank you for living in me and for being my "in-house" counselor and comforter. Guide me into your truth and protect me from the evil one. Teach me how to hear your instruction in the midst of all the noise in the world and follow your leading.

JOURNALING

What are some questions you have about your faith in Christ? How will you pray today for the Holy Spirit to give you greater understanding in these areas?

FOR FURTHER READING

To complete the books of 1, 2, 3 John and Jude during this twelve-part study, read 1 John 4:1–6. For more Bible passages on spiritual discernment, read 1 Kings 3:9; Psalm 82:5; Jeremiah 6:27; Luke 24:25; 1 Corinthians 2:13–14; Ephesians 5:10; 1 Thessalonians 5:21; and Hebrews 5:14.

ALL ABOUT LOVE

God is love. Whoever lives in love lives in God, and God in them.

1 JOHN 4:16

REFLECTION

Love. Can you think of any word that is more misused and more misunderstood? We say we "love our spouse" in the same breath we say we "love *nachos*." How would *you* define love? (Try to avoid any tired descriptions and put a new spin on this mysterious entity!)

SITUATION

John has called on believers to not just accept everything they hear people say about Jesus, but to actually *test* that teaching (and rely on the Holy Spirit's guidance) to determine if it is actually true. In this next section, John again discusses the primary trait that separates those who know God from those who do not: *love.* As John notes, "God is love" (verse 16). Once we experience that love firsthand, it changes our outlook on life and motivates us to share it with others.

OBSERVATION

*Read 1 John 4:7–21 from the New International
Version or the New King James Version.*

NEW INTERNATIONAL VERSION

[7] Dear friends, let us love one another, for love comes from God. Everyone who loves has been born of God and knows God. [8] Whoever does not love does not know God, because God is love. [9] This is how God showed his love among us: He sent his one and only Son into the world that we might live through him. [10] This is love: not that we loved God, but that he loved us and sent his Son as an atoning sacrifice for our sins. [11] Dear friends, since God so loved us, we also ought to love one another. [12] No one has ever seen God; but if we love one another, God lives in us and his love is made complete in us.

[13] This is how we know that we live in him and he in us: He has given us of his Spirit. [14] And we have seen and testify that the Father has sent his Son to be the Savior of the world. [15] If anyone acknowledges that Jesus is the Son of God, God lives in them and they in God. [16] And so we know and rely on the love God has for us.

God is love. Whoever lives in love lives in God, and God in them. [17] This is how love is made complete among us so that we will have confidence on the day of judgment: In this world we are like Jesus. [18] There is no fear in love. But perfect love drives out fear, because fear has to do with punishment. The one who fears is not made perfect in love.

[19] We love because he first loved us. [20] Whoever claims to love God yet hates a brother or sister is a liar. For whoever does not love their brother and sister, whom they have seen, cannot love God, whom they have not seen. [21] And he has given us this command: Anyone who loves God must also love their brother and sister.

NEW KING JAMES VERSION

[7] Beloved, let us love one another, for love is of God; and everyone who loves is born of God and knows God. [8] He who does not love does not

know God, for God is love. [9] In this the love of God was manifested toward us, that God has sent His only begotten Son into the world, that we might live through Him. [10] In this is love, not that we loved God, but that He loved us and sent His Son to be the propitiation for our sins. [11] Beloved, if God so loved us, we also ought to love one another.

[12] No one has seen God at any time. If we love one another, God abides in us, and His love has been perfected in us. [13] By this we know that we abide in Him, and He in us, because He has given us of His Spirit. [14] And we have seen and testify that the Father has sent the Son as Savior of the world. [15] Whoever confesses that Jesus is the Son of God, God abides in him, and he in God. [16] And we have known and believed the love that God has for us. God is love, and he who abides in love abides in God, and God in him.

[17] Love has been perfected among us in this: that we may have boldness in the day of judgment; because as He is, so are we in this world. [18] There is no fear in love; but perfect love casts out fear, because fear involves torment. But he who fears has not been made perfect in love. [19] We love Him because He first loved us.

[20] If someone says, "I love God," and hates his brother, he is a liar; for he who does not love his brother whom he has seen, how can he love God whom he has not seen? [21] And this commandment we have from Him: that he who loves God must love his brother also.

EXPLORATION

1. According to this passage, what is the connection between *God* and *love*?

---

2. What is love—an emotion, an action, a commitment, or something else? Explain.

3. How does John say that God demonstrated his love?

4. Can a person truly receive love without somehow passing it on? Why or why not?

5. How does a Christian demonstrate love for God?

6. What does John mean when he argues there is "no fear in love" (verse 18)?

INSPIRATION

The prophet Isaiah says that sin has left us as lost and confused as stray sheep. "We all, like sheep, have gone astray, each of us has turned to our own way" (Isaiah 53:6). If the prophet had known one of my dogs, he might have written, "All we like *Molly* have gone astray . . . "

For such a sweet dog, she had a stubborn, defiant streak. Once her nose got wind of a neighbor's grilling steak or uncovered trash, no amount of commands could control her. You don't want to know how many times this minister chased that dog down the street, tossing un-minister-like warnings at his pet. She "sinned," living as if her master didn't exist. She was known to wander.

One time, we thought she'd wandered away for good. We posted her picture on bulletin boards, drove through the neighborhood, calling her name. Finally, after a day of futility, I went to the animal shelter. I described Molly to the animal shelter director. She wished me luck and pointed toward a barrack-shaped building whose door bore the sign "Stray Dogs."

Warning to softhearted dog lovers: don't go there! I've not seen such sadness since they shut down the drive-in movie theater in my hometown. Cage after cage of longing, frightened eyes. Big, round ones. Narrow, dark ones. Some peered from beneath the thick eyebrows of Cocker Spaniel. Others from the bald-as-a-rock head of a Chihuahua. Different breeds but same plight. Lost as blind geese with no clue how to get home. . . .

I didn't find Molly at the shelter. I did have a crazy urge at the shelter, however. I wanted to announce Jesus' declaration: "Be of good cheer. You are lost no more!" I wanted to take the strays home with me, to unlock door after door and fill my car with barking, tail-wagging dogs. I didn't do it. As much as I wanted to save the dogs, I wanted to stay married even more.

But I did have the urge, and the urge helps me understand why Jesus made forgiveness his first fearless announcement. Yes, we have disappointed God. But, no, God has not abandoned us. . . . Jesus loves us too much to leave us in doubt about his grace. His "perfect love drives out fear" (1 John 4:18).

If God loved with an imperfect love, we would have high cause to worry. Imperfect love keeps a list of sins and consults it often. But God keeps no list of our wrongs. His love casts out fear because he casts out our sin! (From *Fearless* by Max Lucado.)

REACTION

7. How have you witnessed the truth of the prophet's statement that "we all, like sheep, have gone astray" (Isaiah 53:6)?

---

8. What are some "Molly moments" you've had in your life? How did God find you?

---

9. Why is it significant that *God* is the one who first pursued you?

10. What are some practical ways you can know if you are growing in God's love?

11. In their more honest moments, some Christians confess, "I know in my head that God loves me, but I don't always sense it in my heart." What counsel would you give such a person?

12. Do you think it is easier to love God or other people? Why?

LIFE LESSONS

All too often, we embrace an overly sentimental view of love. We see love as lots of hugging and glossing over hurtful actions or unpleasant realities. To be sure, God's love is accepting and forgiving. But it is also stern, and therein lies the great mystery. God loves us *just as* we are, but he also loves us too much to *leave us* as we are. God's love is transforming and redemptive, which means it's disruptive and uncomfortable. We need to remember this as both experience and export God's love. The love of God is pure and always governed by truth. If we are to be imitators of God, our love for others will have to be tough and uncompromising.

DEVOTION

God of love, it is a miracle that you sought us where we were and rescued us. Thank you for the continued love you show in not allowing us to remain stagnant and where we are. Help us to embrace your love and demonstrate it to other. Let your goodness fill our lives and spill over.

JOURNALING

List seven people with whom you interact regularly. Next to each name, write a specific way how you can and *will* demonstrate God's love to that person during the upcoming week.

FOR FURTHER READING

To complete the books of 1, 2, 3 John and Jude during this twelve-part study, read 1 John 4:7–21. For more Bible passages on love, read Deuteronomy 7:6–8; Psalm 146:8; Jeremiah 31:3; John 3:16–17; Romans 5:8; 1 Corinthians 13:4–8; Ephesians 2:4–5; and Jude 1:21.

THE VICTORIOUS LIFE

*This is the victory that has overcome the world—
our faith. . . . He who overcomes the world . . .
believes that Jesus is the Son of God.*

1 JOHN 54:4–5 NKJV

REFLECTION

Acing the test. Getting the trophy. Winning the account. Garnering the promotion. Our society is built on fierce competition . . . and to the victors belong the spoils. What have been the greatest achievements or proudest accomplishments so far in your life?

_____

_____

_____

_____

_____

_____

_____

_____

_____

_____

_____

_____

SITUATION

John has just concluded a prolonged discussion on the love of God and how we can recognize those who belong to him by the love of God they show to others. John now expounds on this idea by showing that those who have _faith_ in Jesus likewise belong to God. John acknowledges that as believers in Christ, we have a real and powerful enemy who seeks to surround us with deceptive ideologies. However, we do not need to fear, because we can know we _belong_ to God, and we have put our faith in the One who "overcomes the world" (verse 5). Our trust is in the victorious Christ who defeated death and the grave. We are spiritual conquerors!

OBSERVATION

Read 1 John 5:1–5 from the New International
Version or the New King James Version.

NEW INTERNATIONAL VERSION

5 Everyone who believes that Jesus is the Christ is born of God, and everyone who loves the father loves his child as well. 2 This is how we know that we love the children of God: by loving God and carrying out his commands. 3 In fact, this is love for God: to keep his commands. And his commands are not burdensome, 4 for everyone born of God overcomes the world. This is the victory that has overcome the world, even our faith. 5 Who is it that overcomes the world? Only the one who believes that Jesus is the Son of God.

NEW KING JAMES VERSION

5 Whoever believes that Jesus is the Christ is born of God, and everyone who loves Him who begot also loves him who is begotten of Him. 2 By this we know that we love the children of God, when we love God and keep His commandments. 3 For this is the love of God, that we keep His commandments. And His commandments are not burdensome. 4 For whatever is born of God overcomes the world. And this is the victory that has overcome the world—our faith. 5 Who is he who overcomes the world, but he who believes that Jesus is the Son of God?

EXPLORATION

1. Do you think there are a lot of pretenders in church—people with insincere faith? Why or why not?

2. What distinguishes true and saving faith from spurious faith?

3. John says that "God's commands are not burdensome" (verse 3). Do you agree with this statement? Why or why not?

4. Read Matthew 11:28–30. What does Jesus say about "yoke"? How does this relate to what John is saying in this passage?

5. Believers often talk about living "a victorious Christian life." What does that actually mean?

6. Even today, Christians suffer persecution at the hands of others. Given this, how can John claim that being a child of God gives you victory over the world?

_____

_____

_____

_____

_____

INSPIRATION

Some expectations sputter and flop like an untied balloon. Remember the shining-armor boyfriend who became the heartbreaking two-timer? The fast-track promotion that landed you in the forgotten basement cubicle? The cross-country move you made to "find yourself"? You found yourself, all right. You found yourself with higher rent and fewer friends.

"If only" dreams lurk in each biography. "If only I could find a mate . . . a career . . . a bright red, affordable '65 Mustang." The only barrier between you and bliss is an "if only." Sometimes you cross it. You find the mate or the career or the Mustang and . . . you count the disappointments and sigh.

Life has letdowns. And how do you know Christ won't be one of them? Honestly. Dare you believe that he gives what he promises to give? Life. Eternal life. "Whoever believes in him shall not perish but have eternal life" (John 3:16). We need to ponder this word: _life_.

Beer companies offer you life in their hops. Perfume makers promise new life for your romance. But don't confuse costume jewelry with God's sapphire.

Jesus offers _zoe_, the Greek word for "life as God has it." Whereas _bios_, its sibling term, is life extensive, _zoe_ is life intensive. Jesus talks less about life's duration and more about its quality, vitality, energy, and fulfillment. What the new mate, sports car, or unexpected check could never do, Christ says, "I can.". . .

Others offer life, but no one offers to do what Jesus does—to reconnect us to his power. But how can we know? How do we know that Jesus knows what he's talking about? The ultimate answer, according to his flagship followers, is the vacated tomb. . . .

Can Jesus actually replace death with life? He did a convincing job with his own. And we can trust him because he has been there. (From *3:16: The Numbers of Hope* by Max Lucado.)

REACTION

7. How can you know that Jesus will give you the victorious life that he promises?

_____

_____

_____

_____

8. How would you describe the difference between victory in Christ and victory in the world?

_____

_____

_____

_____

9. In what way is obedience tied to victorious living?

_____

_____

_____

10. What are some spiritual world-conquering victories that you have experienced?

_____

_____

_____

11. Some Christians claim to have faith but experience dull and ordinary lives. Others claim to have faith and live lives of adventure and excitement. What makes the difference?

_____

_____

_____

12. What are the great obstacles facing you now that you need to overcome? What are some steps of faith God is calling you to take?

_____

_____

_____

LIFE LESSONS

Be careful. Be _very_ careful. Things are almost never what they seem. See that squawling infant in the fly-infested stable? He's actually the Creator of the cosmos. And when he grows up, this carpenter-turned-rabbi will say, "Want to be great? Bend low and wash the feet of others. Want to gain everything? You can, by giving up everything. Got enemies? Love them." How topsy-turvy this kingdom of Christ! We forgive those who hurt us. We rejoice in suffering. We laugh in the face of death, because not even the deep darkness at Golgotha on Friday afternoon can stop the great celebration at the empty tomb on Sunday morning. Spiritual triumph is *not* a foolish wish. Christians have victory because they serve a risen Savior and coming King.

DEVOTION

Lord Jesus, you have given us the ultimate victory in your death and by your resurrection. You have defeated all of our enemies—sin, death, and the devil himself. Help us to recognize the victory you given us so we can live as true overcomers. Let us live in your glorious triumph today.

JOURNALING

If you were the enemy, what vulnerabilities would you exploit in your life? What does this tell you about where you need to fortify your spiritual defenses?

FOR FURTHER READING

To complete the books of 1, 2, 3 John and Jude during this twelve-part study, read 1 John 5:1–5. For more Bible passages on victory in Christ, read Psalm 44:5; Luke 10:19; John 16:33; Romans 8:35–37; 1 Corinthians 15:24; Colossians 2:13–15; and Revelation 3:21; 6:2; 17:14.

LESSON EIGHT

ETERNAL LIFE
IN CHRIST

*I write these things to you who believe in
the name of the Son of God so that you
may know that you have eternal life.*

1 JOHN 5:13

REFLECTION

It has been estimated that perhaps as many as half of all churchgoers do not possess the assurance of their salvation. In other words, they cannot say for sure whether they will spend eternity with God in heaven. Why do you think so few believers have this assurance?

_____

_____

_____

_____

_____

_____

_____

_____

_____

_____

_____

SITUATION

John has been writing to a community of beleaguered believers who were being subjected to competing claims about Jesus—who he really was and who he claimed to be. In this final section, he concludes his arguments by stating Jesus "came by water and blood" (verse 6)—something John observed personally at the crucifixion when "one of the soldiers pierced Jesus' side with a spear, bringing a sudden flow of blood and water" (John 19:34). John was a witness that Jesus died a physical death (and rose again), and the Holy Spirit at work in the church has "testified" to this truth as well. The truth is clear: Jesus really _is_ who he claimed to be, and those who trust in him really _can_ look forward to a life that never ends!

OBSERVATION

*Read 1 John 5:6–13 from the New International
Version or the New King James Version.*

NEW INTERNATIONAL VERSION

[6] This is the one who came by water and blood—Jesus Christ. He did not come by water only, but by water and blood. And it is the Spirit who testifies, because the Spirit is the truth. [7] For there are three that testify: [8] the Spirit, the water and the blood; and the three are in agreement. [9] We accept human testimony, but God's testimony is greater because it is the testimony of God, which he has given about his Son. [10] Whoever believes in the Son of God accepts this testimony. Whoever does not believe God has made him out to be a liar, because they have not believed the testimony God has given about his Son. [11] And this is the testimony: God has given us eternal life, and this life is in his Son. [12] Whoever has the Son has life; whoever does not have the Son of God does not have life.

[13] I write these things to you who believe in the name of the Son of God so that you may know that you have eternal life.

NEW KING JAMES VERSION

[6] This is He who came by water and blood—Jesus Christ; not only by water, but by water and blood. And it is the Spirit who bears witness, because the Spirit is truth. [7] For there are three that bear witness in heaven: the Father, the Word, and the Holy Spirit; and these three are one. [8] And there are three that bear witness on earth: the Spirit, the water, and the blood; and these three agree as one.

[9] If we receive the witness of men, the witness of God is greater; for this is the witness of God which He has testified of His Son. [10] He who believes in the Son of God has the witness in himself; he who does not believe God has made Him a liar, because he has not believed the testimony that God has given of His Son. [11] And this is the testimony: that God has given us eternal life, and this life is in His Son. [12] He who has

the Son has life; he who does not have the Son of God does not have life. ¹³ These things I have written to you who believe in the name of the Son of God, that you may know that you have eternal life, and that you may continue to believe in the name of the Son of God.

EXPLORATION

1. Some of the false teachers in John's day were saying God's Spirit only came on Jesus at his water baptism and then departed at his bloody death. How does this shed light on verses 6–8?

2. How can you be sure that Jesus really *was* and *is* the Messiah?

3. What would you say to a person who argues there are many ways to God, many paths to eternal life, and all religions are basically saying the same thing using different terminology?

4. The disciple John offered his own "human testimony" of the death and resurrection of Jesus. So why does he say, "God's testimony is greater" (verse 9)? What does he mean by this?

5. What is God's testimony in regard the ultimate destination of his children (see verse 11)?

6. Why is it so important to have this testimony directory from God in the Bible?

INSPIRATION

Sometimes I give away money at the end of a sermon. Not to pay the listeners (though some may feel they've earned it) but to make a point. I offer a dollar to anyone who will accept it. Free money. A gift. I invite anyone who wants the cash to come and take it.

The response is predictable. A pause. Some shuffling of feet. A wife elbows her husband, and he shakes his head. A teen starts to stand and then remembers her reputation. A five-year-old starts walking down the aisle, and his mother pulls him back. Finally, some courageous (or impoverished) soul stands up and says, "I'll take it!" The dollar is given, and the application begins.

"Why didn't you take my offer?" I ask the rest. Some say they were too embarrassed. The pain wasn't worth the gain. Others feared a catch, a trick. And then there are those whose wallets are fat. What's a buck to someone who has hundreds?

Then the obvious follow-up question. "Why don't people accept Christ's free gift?" The answers are similar. Some are too embarrassed. To accept forgiveness is to admit sin, a step we are slow to take. Others fear a trick, a catch. Surely there is some fine print in the Bible. Others think, Who needs forgiveness when you're as good as I am?

The point makes itself. Though grace is available to all, it's accepted by few. Many choose to sit and wait while only a few choose to stand and trust. (From *In the Grip of Grace* by Max Lucado.)

REACTION

7. Why does the free and unconditional nature of the gospel make so many uncomfortable?

_____

_____

_____

8. Read Romans 6:23. What is the difference between "wages" and a "free gift"?

_____

_____

_____

9. How can you know for sure that you have eternal life?

_____

_____

_____

10. Many believers in Christ envision eternal life as something they will get one day when they die. Is that what this passage teaches? Explain.

11. John writes that *"whoever* has the Son has life" (verse 12). What does this say about the way God invites you to follow him in spite of your past?

12. Why is it important for you to be certain about your eternal destiny?

LIFE LESSONS

The gospel is scandalous. *Eternal life with no fine print and no strings attached? All I have to do is believe? Wait . . . don't I have to agree to do certain things? Surely, I have to clean up my act, right?* Not according to John. The outlandish claim here is that eternal life is a gift. In other words, we can never earn it or deserve it. John also says eternal life is found in Christ . . . period. No other religious system will work (see John 14:6 and Acts 4:12). And notice this life is promised—it is guaranteed—to *all* who put their faith in Christ. God doesn't want us guessing or wondering or crossing our fingers. He wants us to know. And the way we know is this: if we are trusting in Jesus, then our salvation is a settled issue.

DEVOTION

God, thank you for your amazing gift of eternal life. Your Word could not be clearer: if we have the Son—if we believe in him—then we have eternal life. Help us to embrace the implications of this truth each day in our lives . . . and give you continual praise for your mercy.

JOURNALING

How sure are you of your salvation? What tends to cause you to doubt it?

FOR FURTHER READING

To complete the books of 1, 2, 3 John and Jude during this twelve-part study, read 1 John 5:6–13. For more Bible passages on the free gift of eternal life, read John 5:24–27; 14:1–4; Romans 3:22–25; 1 Corinthians 2:9; Ephesians 2:8–9; 1 Timothy 1:14–16; and Revelation 7:9–17.

RELATIONSHIP WITH GOD

The Son of God has come and has given us an understanding, that we may know Him who is true; and we are in Him who is true, in His Son Jesus Christ.

1 JOHN 5:20 NKJV

REFLECTION

Every relationship goes through stages—periods of intense intimacy intermingled with times of distance. Think about history of your fellowship with God. When have you felt closest to him? When have you felt miles away from him? Where are you now?

SITUATION

John concludes his epistle with a reminder of the privileges true believers enjoy—the ability to approach God and know that he will hear us. He notes that just as Jesus is concerned about us and is our "advocate with the Father" (2:1), so we should be concerned about our fellow believers who sin and intercede for them in prayer. John ends by telling his readers to keep themselves from idols, which likely refers to the doctrine of the false teachers. Likewise, they are to avoid the "sin that leads to death," or following doctrine that leads away from the truth they have received of Christ. What matters most is living by simple trust in a great God.

OBSERVATION

Read 1 John 5:14–21 from the New International Version or the New King James Version.

NEW INTERNATIONAL VERSION

[14] This is the confidence we have in approaching God: that if we ask anything according to his will, he hears us. [15] And if we know that he hears us—whatever we ask—we know that we have what we asked of him.

[16] If you see any brother or sister commit a sin that does not lead to death, you should pray and God will give them life. I refer to those whose sin does not lead to death. There is a sin that leads to death. I am not saying that you should pray about that. [17] All wrongdoing is sin, and there is sin that does not lead to death.

[18] We know that anyone born of God does not continue to sin; the One who was born of God keeps them safe, and the evil one cannot harm them. [19] We know that we are children of God, and that the whole world is under the control of the evil one. [20] We know also that the Son of God has come and has given us understanding, so that we may know him who is true. And we are in him who is true by being in his Son Jesus Christ. He is the true God and eternal life.

[21] Dear children, keep yourselves from idols.

NEW KING JAMES VERSION

[14] Now this is the confidence that we have in Him, that if we ask anything according to His will, He hears us. [15] And if we know that He hears us, whatever we ask, we know that we have the petitions that we have asked of Him.

[16] If anyone sees his brother sinning a sin which does not lead to death, he will ask, and He will give him life for those who commit sin not leading to death. There is sin leading to death. I do not say that he should pray about that. [17] All unrighteousness is sin, and there is sin not leading to death.

¹⁸ We know that whoever is born of God does not sin; but he who has been born of God keeps himself, and the wicked one does not touch him.

¹⁹ We know that we are of God, and the whole world lies under the sway of the wicked one.

²⁰ And we know that the Son of God has come and has given us an understanding, that we may know Him who is true; and we are in Him who is true, in His Son Jesus Christ. This is the true God and eternal life.

²¹ Little children, keep yourselves from idols. Amen.

EXPLORATION

1. How can you be sure that God will hear and answer your prayers?

_____

_____

_____

_____

_____

_____

_____

2. What does it mean to ask things from God "according to his will" (verse 1)? Why is this an important distinction in receiving answers to your prayers?

_____

_____

_____

_____

_____

_____

_____

3. Read Ephesians 3:12 and Hebrews 4:16. How do these verses agree with what John is instructing believers regarding prayer in this passage?

4. What does living in fellowship with God and others require of you when you observe that a fellow Christian is living in sin?

5. How do we reconcile the statement that "the evil one cannot harm" God's children (verse 18) with the reality that Christians everywhere still struggle with sin?

6. Why do you think John closes with a warning about idolatry (see verse 21)?

INSPIRATION

God wants to be as close to us as a branch is to a vine. One is an extension of the other. It's impossible to tell where one starts and the other ends. The branch isn't connected only at the moment of bearing fruit. The gardener doesn't keep the branches in a box and then, on the day he wants grapes, glue them to the vine. No, the branch constantly draws nutrition from the vine. Separation means certain death.

God also uses the temple to depict the intimacy he desires. "Do you not know," Paul writes, "that your bodies are temples of the Holy Spirit, who is in you, whom you have received from God?" (1 Corinthians 6:19). Think with me about the temple for a moment. Was God a visitor or a resident in Solomon's temple? Would you describe his presence as occasional or permanent? You know the answer. God didn't come and go, appear and disappear. He was a permanent presence, always available.

What incredibly good news for us! We are *never* away from God! He is *never* away from us—not even for a moment! God doesn't come to us on Sunday mornings and then exit on Sunday afternoons. He remains within us, continually present in our lives.

The biblical analogy of marriage is the third picture of this encouraging truth. Aren't we the bride of Christ (see Revelation 21:2)? Aren't we united with him (see Romans 6:5)? Haven't we made vows to him, and hasn't he made vows to us? . . .

Can we consider one last analogy from the Bible? How about the sheep with the shepherd? Many times Scripture calls us the flock of God. "We are his people, the sheep of his pasture" (Psalm 100:3). We needn't know much about sheep to know that the shepherd never leaves the flock. If we see a flock coming down the path, we know a shepherd is nearby. If we see a Christian ahead, we can know the same. The Good Shepherd never leaves his sheep. "Even though I walk through the darkest valley, I will fear no evil, for you are with me (Psalm 23:4).

God is as near to you as the vine is to the branch, as present within you as God was in the temple, as intimate with you as a husband with a wife, and as devoted to you as a shepherd to his sheep. (From *Just Like Jesus* by Max Lucado.)

REACTION

7. How much stock should believers put in feelings—as in *feeling* close to God or *sensing* his presence? Why?

8. How can you know your prayers for others are significant?

9. Is it difficult for you to pray with confidence? If so, why do you think that is the case?

10. What are some surefire prayer requests you could or should be making—things you already know God wants?

11. When are some times you have sensed the Lord keeping you safe from sin?

12. An *idol* can represent anything that comes in your life to take the place of God. What people or things or activities threaten to rival God in your life?

LIFE LESSONS

All kinds of things in this world clamor for our attention, affection, and allegiance. And here's the bottom-line truth: to whatever or whomever we allocate our best time, energy, and resources, *that* is what or whom we worship. John's first epistle reminds us that God is the only one worthy of all that we are and have. Nothing matters more than cultivating a rich relationship with him that changes us and moves us to love and serve others. No wonder John counsels us to beware getting sidetracked—to watch out for teachings that diminish Christ's glory and look out for idols that tempt us to take our gaze off Jesus.

DEVOTION

Lord, you offer us yourself. What a privilege—to walk with you and know you and be one with you. Keep us from wandering like sheep who have gone astray. Draw our heart into yours. Grant us the riches of having true fellowship with you!

JOURNALING

What are some specific things that you need to pray about with confidence today?

FOR FURTHER READING

To complete the books of 1, 2, 3 John and Jude during this twelve-part study, read 1 John 5:14–21. For more Bible passages on drawing near to God, read 2 Chronicles 7:13–15; Psalm 27:4; John 6:43–45; 15:1–10; Ephesians 5:19–31; Hebrews 10:19–22; James 4:8–10; and Revelation 3:20.

LESSON TEN

TRUTH *AND* LOVE

And this is love: that we walk in obedience to [God's] commands. As you have heard from the beginning, his command is that you walk in love.

2 JOHN 1:6

REFLECTION

Truth *and* love. Think of a time when you had to express a hard truth to a person you loved. What made it difficult to express that truth? How were you able to do so in a loving manner?

_____

_____

_____

_____

_____

_____

_____

_____

_____

_____

_____

_____

_____

_____

_____

_____

_____

_____

SITUATION

In John's second letter, an inspired "postcard" to believers, he stresses the relationship between *love* and *truth*. He begins by rejoicing in the fact so many of the believers are "walking in the truth" (verse 4), but he wants them to keep showing love to one another by "[walking] in obedience" to God's commands (verse 6). John also desires the believers to continue embracing the truth by not being deceived by false teachers in the church. He thus advises them to reject anyone who "does not bring this teaching" they have received from him (verse 11), so they will go the distance in the race of faith. For John, there is no divine love apart from the truth of God—the two go hand in hand together!

OBSERVATION

Read 2 John 1–13 from the New International Version or the New King James Version.

New International Version

¹ The elder,

To the lady chosen by God and to her children, whom I love in the truth—and not I only, but also all who know the truth— ² because of the truth, which lives in us and will be with us forever:

³ Grace, mercy and peace from God the Father and from Jesus Christ, the Father's Son, will be with us in truth and love.

⁴ It has given me great joy to find some of your children walking in the truth, just as the Father commanded us. ⁵ And now, dear lady, I am not writing you a new command but one we have had from the beginning. I ask that we love one another. ⁶ And this is love: that we walk in obedience to his commands. As you have heard from the beginning, his command is that you walk in love.

⁷ I say this because many deceivers, who do not acknowledge Jesus Christ as coming in the flesh, have gone out into the world. Any such person is the deceiver and the antichrist. ⁸ Watch out that you do not lose what we have worked for, but that you may be rewarded fully. ⁹ Anyone who runs ahead and does not continue in the teaching of Christ does not have God; whoever continues in the teaching has both the Father and the Son. ¹⁰ If anyone comes to you and does not bring this teaching, do not take them into your house or welcome them. ¹¹ Anyone who welcomes them shares in their wicked work.

[12] I have much to write to you, but I do not want to use paper and ink. Instead, I hope to visit you and talk with you face to face, so that our joy may be complete.

[13] The children of your sister, who is chosen by God, send their greetings.

NEW KING JAMES VERSION

[1] The Elder,

To the elect lady and her children, whom I love in truth, and not only I, but also all those who have known the truth, [2] because of the truth which abides in us and will be with us forever:

[3] Grace, mercy, and peace will be with you from God the Father and from the Lord Jesus Christ, the Son of the Father, in truth and love.

[4] I rejoiced greatly that I have found some of your children walking in truth, as we received commandment from the Father. [5] And now I plead with you, lady, not as though I wrote a new commandment to you, but that which we have had from the beginning: that we love one another. [6] This is love, that we walk according to His commandments. This is the commandment, that as you have heard from the beginning, you should walk in it.

[7] For many deceivers have gone out into the world who do not confess Jesus Christ as coming in the flesh. This is a deceiver and an antichrist. [8] Look to yourselves, that we do not lose those things we worked for, but that we may receive a full reward.

[9] Whoever transgresses and does not abide in the doctrine of Christ does not have God. He who abides in the doctrine of Christ has both the Father and the Son. [10] If anyone comes to you and does not bring this doctrine, do not receive him into your house nor greet him; [11] for he who greets him shares in his evil deeds.

[12] Having many things to write to you, I did not wish to do so with paper and ink; but I hope to come to you and speak face to face, that our joy may be full.

[13] The children of your elect sister greet you. Amen.

EXPLORATION

1. Why is it significant that John uses the word *truth* five times in the first four verses?

2. How would answer those who claim, "Your truth is your truth; and my truth is my truth"?

3. Read Matthew 22:36–40. Why is love so fundamental in the life of a believer?

4. John notes "many deceivers have gone out into the world who do not confess Jesus Christ as coming in the flesh" (verse 7). Why is the doctrine of the humanity of Christ so important?

5. To what is John referring when warns his readers not to "lose those things we worked for" (verse 8 NKJV)?

6. "Walk in love" (verse 6). Easy to say . . . not so easy to do. What does this mean, exactly, and how might obedience to this command vary from one Christian to the next?

INSPIRATION

Don't forget, love is a fruit. Step into the orchard of God's work, and what is the first fruit you see? "*Love,* joy, peace, forbearance, kindness, goodness, faithfulness, gentleness and self-control" (Galatians 5:22–23, emphasis added).

Love is a fruit. A fruit of whom? Of your hard work? Of your deep faith? Of your rigorous resolve? No. Love is a fruit of the Spirit of God. . . .

And, this is so important, you are a branch on the vine of God. "I am the vine; you are the branches" (John 15:5). Need a refresher course on how vines function? What is the role of the branch in the bearing of fruit? Branches don't exert a lot of energy. You never hear of gardeners treating branches for exhaustion. Branches don't attend clinics on stress management. Nor do they groan and grunt: "I've got to get this grape out. I've got to get this grape out. I'm going to bear this grape if it kills me!"

No, the branch does none of that. The branch has one job—to receive nourishment from the vine. And you have one job—to receive nourishment from Jesus. "I am the vine; you are the branches. If you remain in me and I in you, you will bear much fruit; apart from me you can do nothing" (verse 5).

Our Lord gets no argument from us on that last line, does he? We have learned the hard way—apart from him we can't produce a thing. Don't you think it's time we learn what happens if we stay attached?

His job is to bear fruit. Our job is to stay put. The more tightly we are attached to Jesus, the more purely his love can pass through us. And oh, what a love it is! Patient. Kind. Does not envy. Does not boast. Is not proud. (From *A Love Worth Giving* by Max Lucado.)

REACTION

7. What is your role as a member of the "branch" that is connected to the "Vine"?

8. Love is a fruit of the Spirit of God. What does this say about any efforts to "earn" God's love? What does it say about your ability to show love apart from Christ?

9. Do you think others look at you and describe you as "fruitful"? Why or why not?

10. How are you seeking to daily abide "in the teaching of Christ" (verse 9)?

11. Many people see truth and love as opposite—that is, truth is harsh and unyielding, while love is warm and accepting. Do you see these qualities as being in opposition?

12. What are some specific action steps you can take this week to become a greater advocate for truth—to help others in your life find the way of truth?

LIFE LESSONS

John had been right next to Jesus in the Upper Room when the Lord gave his famous discourse on love. Often when we remember Jesus' words, "Everyone will know that you are my disciples, if you love one another" (John 13:35), we are thinking only of the more pleasant aspects of love— serving, sacrificing, helping, or sharing. But included in Christ's profound teaching on love is the previous verse: "As I have loved you, so you must love one another" (verse 34). Loving as Christ loved includes some less pleasant aspects of love—confrontation and correction. We must remember that loving like Christ means we will sometimes be intolerant of sinful and dangerous actions in others. We need to love others enough to tell them the truth.

DEVOTION

Lord, it is easy to embrace a mushy attitude toward love—and to turn away from hard encounters our bite our tongue when we know we should speak up. Give us the courage to speak up with sensitivity and tact when others need jarring truth.

JOURNALING

What are some ways people in your life have spoken the truth to you when you needed it?

FOR FURTHER READING

To complete the books of 1, 2, 3 John and Jude during this twelve-part study, read 2 John 1–13. For more Bible passages on walking in love and truth, read Psalm 26:1–3; 86:11; John 8:31–32; 17:17–19; Romans 1:16–17; 1 Corinthians 13:6–8; Ephesians 4:14–15; 5:1–2; and Hebrews 10:23–24.

IMITATING WHAT IS GOOD

Beloved, do not imitate what is evil, but what is good. He who does good is of God, but he who does evil has not seen God.

3 JOHN 1:11 NKJV

REFLECTION

When children play with their friends, they often like to imitate someone they admire . . . a firefighter, soldier, or even a superhero. Think
about someone whom you greatly admire. What are some ways you have
sought to imitate the positive traits you find in that person?

SITUATION

In John's third letter, he points out two specific individuals in the church
for their behavior—but for two very different reasons. On the one hand,
he praises the works of Gaius, a church elder, who repeatedly demon-
strates hospitality and generosity to traveling Christian workers. But on

the other hand, he condemns the actions of Diotrephes, a controlling troublemaker, who has not only stopped other believers for showing hospitality but also kicked them out of the church. John wants Gaius to keep imitating what is good—and to continue showing hospitality by receiving his coworker Demetrius, who will be bearing this letter.

OBSERVATION

Read 3 John 1–14 from the New International Version or the New King James Version.

NEW INTERNATIONAL VERSION

[1] The elder,

To my dear friend Gaius, whom I love in the truth.

[2] Dear friend, I pray that you may enjoy good health and that all may go well with you, even as your soul is getting along well. [3] It gave me great joy when some believers came and testified about your faithfulness to the truth, telling how you continue to walk in it. [4] I have no greater joy than to hear that my children are walking in the truth.

[5] Dear friend, you are faithful in what you are doing for the brothers and sisters, even though they are strangers to you. [6] They have told the church about your love. Please send them on their way in a manner that honors God. [7] It was for the sake of the Name that they went out, receiving no help from the pagans. [8] We ought therefore to show hospitality to such people so that we may work together for the truth.

[9] I wrote to the church, but Diotrephes, who loves to be first, will not welcome us. [10] So when I come, I will call attention to what he is doing, spreading malicious nonsense about us. Not satisfied with that, he even refuses to welcome other believers. He also stops those who want to do so and puts them out of the church.

[11] Dear friend, do not imitate what is evil but what is good. Anyone who does what is good is from God. Anyone who does what is evil has not seen God. [12] Demetrius is well spoken of by everyone—and even by

the truth itself. We also speak well of him, and you know that our testimony is true.

¹³ I have much to write you, but I do not want to do so with pen and ink. ¹⁴ I hope to see you soon, and we will talk face to face.

Peace to you. The friends here send their greetings. Greet the friends there by name.

New King James Version

¹ The Elder,

To the beloved Gaius, whom I love in truth:

² Beloved, I pray that you may prosper in all things and be in health, just as your soul prospers. ³ For I rejoiced greatly when brethren came and testified of the truth that is in you, just as you walk in the truth. ⁴ I have no greater joy than to hear that my children walk in truth.

⁵ Beloved, you do faithfully whatever you do for the brethren and for strangers, ⁶ who have borne witness of your love before the church. If you send them forward on their journey in a manner worthy of God, you will do well, ⁷ because they went forth for His name's sake, taking nothing from the Gentiles. ⁸ We therefore ought to receive such, that we may become fellow workers for the truth.

⁹ I wrote to the church, but Diotrephes, who loves to have the preeminence among them, does not receive us. ¹⁰ Therefore, if I come, I will call to mind his deeds which he does, prating against us with malicious words. And not content with that, he himself does not receive the brethren, and forbids those who wish to, putting them out of the church.

¹¹ Beloved, do not imitate what is evil, but what is good. He who does good is of God, but he who does evil has not seen God.

¹² Demetrius has a good testimony from all, and from the truth itself. And we also bear witness, and you know that our testimony is true.

¹³ I had many things to write, but I do not wish to write to you with pen and ink; ¹⁴ but I hope to see you shortly, and we shall speak face to face.

Peace to you. Our friends greet you. Greet the friends by name.

EXPLORATION

1. If a group of Christians reported on your life—as some apparently did on Gaius's life—what do you think they would say? Why?

2. What does John say was his greatest joy?

3. How would you define *hospitality*?

4. Why is hospitality such an important quality for Christians to possess?

5. Have you known a Diotrephes? Do you agree with John's approach to dealing with him?

6. Why do you think so many people insist on doing things their way rather than God's way—even when they know God's way is ultimately better for them?

INSPIRATION

Reduce the human job description down to one phrase, and this is it: Reflect God's glory. As Paul wrote: "And we, with our unveiled faces reflecting like mirrors the brightness of the Lord, all grow brighter and brighter as we are turned into the image that we reflect; this is the work of the Lord who is Spirit" (2 Corinthians 3:18 TJB).

Some reader just arched an eyebrow. *Wait a second,* you are thinking. *I've read that passage before, more than once. And it sounded different.* Indeed it may have. Perhaps it's because you are used to reading it in a different translation. "But we all, with unveiled face, *beholding as in a mirror* the glory of the Lord, are being transformed into the same image from glory to glory, just as from the Lord, the Spirit" (NKJV, emphasis added).

One translation says, "beholding as in a mirror," another says, "reflecting like mirrors." One implies contemplation. The other implies refraction. Which is accurate?

Actually, both. The verb *katoptrizo* can be translated either way. Translators are in both camps: "with unveiled face, *beholding* as in a mirror" (NKJV); "with our unveiled faces *reflecting* like mirrors" (TJB). . . .

But which meaning did Paul intend? In the context of the passage, Paul paralleled the Christian experience to the Mount Sinai experience of Moses. After the patriarch *beheld* the glory of God, his face *reflected* the glory of God. . . . *The brightness he saw was the brightness he became.* Beholding led to becoming. Becoming led to reflecting.

Perhaps the answer to the translation question, then, is "yes." Did Paul mean "beholding as in a mirror"? Yes. Did Paul mean "reflecting like a mirror"? Yes.

Could it be that the Holy Spirit intentionally selected a verb that would remind us to do both? To behold God so intently that we can't help but reflect him? (From *It's Not About Me* by Max Lucado.)

REACTION

7. How does Paul point out the connection between *beholding* God's glory and *reflecting* it?

_____

_____

_____

_____

8. Why is it so tempting to live for ourselves instead of reflecting God's glory?

_____

_____

_____

_____

9. In what tangible ways do you demonstrate hospitality and generosity to Christian workers?

_____

_____

_____

10. How does John say he is going to approach Diotrephes when he comes to visit?

11. What is the best way to handle someone like Diotrephes in your life?

12. What does John mean when he calls the believers to "not imitate what is evil but what is good" (verse 11)? How does this apply to your life?

LIFE LESSONS

Say the word *hospitality* and many Christians immediately picture a spacious home straight out of a magazine, ideally with a pool and a lavish guesthouse. (And don't forget elegant gourmet meals served on fine china with crystal goblets and real silver!) All those things are nice, but none of them are necessary for us to welcome others and make them feel loved and special. The key to good hospitality isn't found in externals, like linen tablecloths and exquisitely furnished guest bedrooms, but in qualities like servanthood, a listening ear, and an encouraging word. You can practice hospitality in a 400-square-foot efficiency apartment. Look for ways to open your home and your life to those who are world-weary.

DEVOTION

Father, forgive our tendency to pursue our own self-absorbed agenda. Remind us that your desire is for your people to show hospitality. Give us creativity and sensitivity so we might share what we have with those who truly are in need.

JOURNALING

What are five simple and practical ways that you could practice greater hospitality this week?

FOR FURTHER READING

To complete the books of 1, 2, 3 John and Jude during this twelve-part study, read 3 John 1–14. For more Bible passages on imitating Christ, read Matthew 5:14–16; 1 Corinthians 11:1; Galatians 2:19–21; Ephesians 5:1–2; Philippians 3:17–21; 1 Thessalonians 1:4–7; 1 Peter 2:21–22; and Hebrews 6:12.

LESSON TWELVE

RESPECTING GOD'S AUTHORITY

But you, dear friends, by building yourselves up in your most holy faith and praying in the Holy Spirit, keep yourselves in God's love.
JUDE 1:20–21

REFLECTION

Authority is something we tend to like if we have it over others but not something we tend to like if others exert it over us. How do you deal with the authority figures in your life? When, if ever, has a *lack* of submitting to those in authority caused problems for you?

SITUATION

The particular brand of apostasy Jude addresses in his short (but theologically packed) letter is known as *antinomianism*—the belief that because God extends his grace and forgiveness to people, they no longer are obligated to follow his commands. Jude points out the error of these false teachers and their rejection of God's authority by drawing on the unusual example of Michael, an archangel who would not even slander Satan (presumably because of his former authority) but said, "The Lord rebuke you!" (verse 9). For Jude, the false teachers are like Cain in his hatred of authority (see Genesis 4), Balaam in his greed (see Numbers 22), and Korah in his rebelliousness (see Numbers 16). They are "wandering stars" (Jude 1:13) and unreliable guides. Jude's message is clear: avoid these teachers and respect God's commands!

OBSERVATION

*Read Jude 1–25 from the New International
Version or the New King James Version.*

NEW INTERNATIONAL VERSION

¹ Jude, a servant of Jesus Christ and a brother of James,

To those who have been called, who are loved in God the Father and kept for Jesus Christ:

² Mercy, peace and love be yours in abundance.

³ Dear friends, although I was very eager to write to you about the salvation we share, I felt compelled to write and urge you to contend for the faith that was once for all entrusted to God's holy people. ⁴ For certain individuals whose condemnation was written about long ago have secretly slipped in among you. They are ungodly people, who pervert the grace of our God into a license for immorality and deny Jesus Christ our only Sovereign and Lord.

⁵ Though you already know all this, I want to remind you that the Lord at one time delivered his people out of Egypt, but later destroyed those who did not believe. ⁶ And the angels who did not keep their positions of authority but abandoned their proper dwelling—these he has kept in darkness, bound with everlasting chains for judgment on the great Day. ⁷ In a similar way, Sodom and Gomorrah and the surrounding towns gave themselves up to sexual immorality and perversion. They serve as an example of those who suffer the punishment of eternal fire.

⁸ In the very same way, on the strength of their dreams these ungodly people pollute their own bodies, reject authority and heap abuse on

celestial beings. [9] But even the archangel Michael, when he was disputing with the devil about the body of Moses, did not himself dare to condemn him for slander but said, "The Lord rebuke you!" [10] Yet these people slander whatever they do not understand, and the very things they do understand by instinct—as irrational animals do—will destroy them.

[11] Woe to them! They have taken the way of Cain; they have rushed for profit into Balaam's error; they have been destroyed in Korah's rebellion.

[12] These people are blemishes at your love feasts, eating with you without the slightest qualm—shepherds who feed only themselves. They are clouds without rain, blown along by the wind; autumn trees, without fruit and uprooted—twice dead. [13] They are wild waves of the sea, foaming up their shame; wandering stars, for whom blackest darkness has been reserved forever.

[14] Enoch, the seventh from Adam, prophesied about them: "See, the Lord is coming with thousands upon thousands of his holy ones [15] to judge everyone, and to convict all of them of all the ungodly acts they have committed in their ungodliness, and of all the defiant words ungodly sinners have spoken against him." [16] These people are grumblers and faultfinders; they follow their own evil desires; they boast about themselves and flatter others for their own advantage.

[17] But, dear friends, remember what the apostles of our Lord Jesus Christ foretold. [18] They said to you, "In the last times there will be scoffers who will follow their own ungodly desires." [19] These are the people who divide you, who follow mere natural instincts and do not have the Spirit.

[20] But you, dear friends, by building yourselves up in your most holy faith and praying in the Holy Spirit, [21] keep yourselves in God's love as you wait for the mercy of our Lord Jesus Christ to bring you to eternal life.

[22] Be merciful to those who doubt; [23] save others by snatching them from the fire; to others show mercy, mixed with fear—hating even the clothing stained by corrupted flesh.

[24] To him who is able to keep you from stumbling and to present you before his glorious presence without fault and with great joy— [25] to

the only God our Savior be glory, majesty, power and authority, through Jesus Christ our Lord, before all ages, now and forevermore! Amen.

NEW KING JAMES VERSION

[1] Jude, a bondservant of Jesus Christ, and brother of James,

To those who are called, sanctified by God the Father, and preserved in Jesus Christ:

[2] Mercy, peace, and love be multiplied to you.

[3] Beloved, while I was very diligent to write to you concerning our common salvation, I found it necessary to write to you exhorting you to contend earnestly for the faith which was once for all delivered to the saints. [4] For certain men have crept in unnoticed, who long ago were marked out for this condemnation, ungodly men, who turn the grace of our God into lewdness and deny the only Lord God and our Lord Jesus Christ.

[5] But I want to remind you, though you once knew this, that the Lord, having saved the people out of the land of Egypt, afterward destroyed those who did not believe. [6] And the angels who did not keep their proper domain, but left their own abode, He has reserved in everlasting chains under darkness for the judgment of the great day; [7] as Sodom and Gomorrah, and the cities around them in a similar manner to these, having given themselves over to sexual immorality and gone after strange flesh, are set forth as an example, suffering the vengeance of eternal fire.

[8] Likewise also these dreamers defile the flesh, reject authority, and speak evil of dignitaries. [9] Yet Michael the archangel, in contending with the devil, when he disputed about the body of Moses, dared not bring against him a reviling accusation, but said, "The Lord rebuke you!" [10] But these speak evil of whatever they do not know; and whatever they know naturally, like brute beasts, in these things they corrupt themselves. [11] Woe to them! For they have gone in the way of Cain, have run greedily in the error of Balaam for profit, and perished in the rebellion of Korah.

¹² These are spots in your love feasts, while they feast with you without fear, serving only themselves. They are clouds without water, carried about by the winds; late autumn trees without fruit, twice dead, pulled up by the roots; ¹³ raging waves of the sea, foaming up their own shame; wandering stars for whom is reserved the blackness of darkness forever.

¹⁴ Now Enoch, the seventh from Adam, prophesied about these men also, saying, "Behold, the Lord comes with ten thousands of His saints, ¹⁵ to execute judgment on all, to convict all who are ungodly among them of all their ungodly deeds which they have committed in an ungodly way, and of all the harsh things which ungodly sinners have spoken against Him."

¹⁶ These are grumblers, complainers, walking according to their own lusts; and they mouth great swelling words, flattering people to gain advantage. ¹⁷ But you, beloved, remember the words which were spoken before by the apostles of our Lord Jesus Christ: ¹⁸ how they told you that there would be mockers in the last time who would walk according to their own ungodly lusts. ¹⁹ These are sensual persons, who cause divisions, not having the Spirit.

²⁰ But you, beloved, building yourselves up on your most holy faith, praying in the Holy Spirit, ²¹ keep yourselves in the love of God, looking for the mercy of our Lord Jesus Christ unto eternal life.

²² And on some have compassion, making a distinction; ²³ but others save with fear, pulling them out of the fire, hating even the garment defiled by the flesh.

> ²⁴ Now to Him who is able to keep you from stumbling,
> And to present you faultless
> Before the presence of His glory with exceeding joy,
> ²⁵ To God our Savior,
> Who alone is wise,
> Be glory and majesty,
> Dominion and power,
> Both now and forever.
> Amen.

EXPLORATION

1. Why did Jude feel compelled to write this urgent letter to the church?

2. In what ways is Jude's ancient epistle timely and relevant to our culture today?

3. Jude speaks frequently about judgment. How does the idea that God will punish unrepentant sinners affect you?

3. What are some examples Jude uses to illustrate God's judgment against sin (see verses 5–7)?

4. How does Jude say the false teachers were rejecting God's authority?

5. What are some subtle ways modern churchgoers weaken the fellowship and ministry of their respective churches?

_____

_____

_____

6. How can Christians know which people in their church are insincere and should be shunned and which ones need mercy (see verse 22)?

_____

_____

INSPIRATION

You and I are on a great climb. The wall is high, and the stakes are higher. You took your first step the day you confessed Christ as the Son of God. He gave you his harness—the Holy Spirit. In your hands he placed a rope—his Word.

Your first steps were confident and strong, but with the journey came weariness, and with the height came fear. You lost your footing. You lost your focus. You lost your grip, and you fell. For a moment, which seemed like forever, you tumbled wildly. Out of control. Out of self-control. Disoriented. Dislodged. Falling.

But then the rope tightened, and the tumble ceased. You hung in the harness and found it to be strong. You grasped the rope and found it to be true. You looked at your guide and found Jesus securing your soul. With a sheepish confession, you smiled at him and he smiled at you, and the journey resumed.

Now you are wiser. You have learned to go slowly. You are careful. You are cautious, but you are also confident. You trust the rope. You rely on the harness.

And though you can't see your guide, you know him. You know he is strong. You know he is able to keep you from falling.

And you know you are only a few more steps from the top. So whatever you do, don't quit. Though your falls are great, his strength is greater. You will make it. You will see the summit. You will stand at the top. And when you get there, the first thing you'll do is join with all the others who have made the climb and sing this verse:

"To him who is able to keep you from stumbling and to present you before his glorious presence without fault and with great joy—to the only God our Savior be glory, majesty, power and authority, through Jesus Christ our Lord, before all ages, now and forevermore! Amen" (Jude 1:24–25). (From *A Gentle Thunder* by Max Lucado.)

REACTION

7. How would you describe the "climb" you are taking in your journey with Christ?

_____

_____

_____

_____

8. Why is it necessary to have a kind of "holy fear" if you are to keep from falling?

_____

_____

_____

9. Jude warns against divisive people in the church (see verse 19). What kinds of attitudes and actions typically create division in a congregation?

_____

_____

_____

10. If you were given the task of trying to help your church in the area of purity (resisting sexual immorality), what specific measures would you implement?

_____

_____

_____

_____

11. What does it mean to "keep yourselves in God's love" (verse 21)?

_____

_____

_____

12. How would you answer a person who argued that sin is not that big a deal because Jesus already paid the price for all our sins?

_____

_____

_____

LIFE LESSONS

The good news of Jesus is more than a set of religious facts or theological propositions. It is the very power of God (see Romans 1:16). When we believe in the gospel, we undergo instant, monumental, and eternal life change. Whether we _feel_ anything or not, salvation makes us fundamentally and essentially different. In that instant of faith, we come alive spiritually. We are transformed (see 2 Corinthians 5:17). Suddenly, we possess a new nature with new desires and new God-given capacities. The goal of the Christian life, then, is to work with God's Spirit to strengthen this new life and allow it to define and shape our lives. And sin? Since it is no longer part of the new, true us, we do not have to listen to it. We are free to live a new life of purity!

DEVOTION

God, thank you for always being present in our lives. Thank you for the strength you provide. Thank you for catching us and guiding us when we feel like we will fall. To you—and you alone—be all the glory, greatness, power, and authority. Be honored in our lives today!

JOURNALING

What evidence do you see in your life that you are respecting God and keeping his commands?

FOR FURTHER READING

To complete the books of 1, 2, 3 John and Jude during this twelve-part study, read Jude 1–25. For more Bible passages on showing respect to God, read Leviticus 19:1–4; Psalm 103:17; Proverbs 8:13; 9:10; 10:27; Matthew 10:26–28; Romans 14:10–12; 1 Timothy 6:11–16; Hebrews 10:26–31; and Revelation 15:4.

LEADER'S GUIDE FOR SMALL GROUPS

Thank you for your willingness to lead a group through *Life Lessons from 1, 2, 3 John and Jude*. The rewards of being a leader are different from those of participating, and we hope you find your own walk with Jesus deepened by this experience. During the twelve lessons in this study, you will guide your group through selected passages in 1, 2, 3 John and Jude and explore the key themes of the letters. There are several elements in this leader's guide that will help you as you structure your study and reflection time, so be sure to follow along and take advantage of each one.

BEFORE YOU BEGIN

Before your first meeting, make sure the group members have their own copy of the *Life Lessons from 1, 2, 3 John and Jude* study guide so they can follow along and have their answers written out ahead of time. Alternately, you can hand out the guides at your first meeting and give the group some time to look over the material and ask any preliminary questions. Be sure to send a sheet around the room during that first meeting and have the members write down their name, phone number, and email address so you can keep in touch with them during the week.

There are two ways to structure the duration of the study. You can choose to cover each lesson individually for a total of twelve weeks of discussion, or you can combine two lessons together per week for a total of six weeks of discussion. (Note that if the group members read the selected passages of Scripture for each lesson, they will cover the entire books of 1, 2, 3 John and Jude during the study.) The following table illustrates these options:

Twelve-Week Format

Week	Lessons Covered	Reading
1	Fellowship with God	1 John 1:1–2:2
2	Obedience to God	1 John 2:3–17
3	Enemies of Christ!	1 John 2:18–29
4	Chips Off the Old Block	1 John 3:1–24
5	Spiritual Discernment	1 John 4:1–6
6	All About Love	1 John 4:7–21
7	The Victorious Life	1 John 5:1–5
8	Eternal Life in Christ	1 John 5:6–13
9	Relationship with God	1 John 5:14–21
10	Truth *and* Love	2 John 1–13
11	Imitating What Is Good	3 John 1–14
12	Respecting God's Authority	Jude 1–25

Six-Week Format

Week	Lessons Covered	Reading
1	Fellowship with God / Obedience to God	1 John 1:1–2:17
2	Enemies of Christ! / Chips Off the Old Block	1 John 2:18–3:24
3	Spiritual Discernment / All About Love	1 John 4:1–21
4	The Victorious Life / Eternal Life in Christ	1 John 5:1–13
5	Relationship with God / Truth *and* Love	1 John 5:14–21; 2 John 1–13
6	Imitating What Is Good / Respecting God's Authority	3 John 1–14; Jude 1–25

Generally, the ideal size you will want for the group is between eight to ten people, which ensures everyone will have enough time to participate in discussions. If you have more people, you might want to break up the main group into smaller subgroups. Encourage those who show up at the first meeting to commit to attending the duration of the study, as this will help the group members get to know each other, create stability for the group, and help you know how to prepare each week.

Each of the lessons begins with a brief reflection that highlights the theme you will be discussing that week. As you begin your group time, have the group members briefly respond to the opening question to get them thinking about the topic at hand. Some people may want to tell a long story in response to one of these questions, but the goal is to keep the answers brief. Ideally, you want everyone in the group to get a chance to answer, so try to keep the responses to just a few minutes. If you have more talkative group members, say up front that everyone needs to limit his or her answer to two minutes.

Give the group members a chance to answer, but tell them to feel free to pass if they wish. With the rest of the study, it's generally not a good idea to have everyone answer every question—a free-flowing discussion is more desirable. But with the opening reflection question, you can go around the circle. Encourage shy people to share, but don't force them.

Before your first meeting, let the group members know how the lessons are broken down. During your group discussion time the members will be drawing on the answers they wrote to the Exploration and Reaction sections, so encourage them to always complete these ahead of time. Also, invite them to bring any questions and insights they uncovered while reading to your next meeting, especially if they had a breakthrough moment or if they didn't understand something they read.

WEEKLY PREPARATION

As the leader, there are a few things you should do to prepare for each meeting:

- *Read through the lesson.* This will help you to become familiar with the content and know how to structure the discussion times.
- *Decide which questions you want to discuss.* Depending on how you structure your group time, you may not be able to cover every question. So select the questions ahead of time that you absolutely want the group to explore.
- *Be familiar with the questions you want to discuss.* When the group meets you'll be watching the clock, so you want to make sure you are familiar with the Bible study questions you have selected. You can then spend time in the passage again when the group meets. In this way, you'll ensure you have the passage more deeply in your mind than your group members.
- *Pray for your group.* Pray for your group members throughout the week and ask God to lead them as they study his Word.
- *Bring extra supplies to your meeting.* The members should bring their own pens for writing notes, but it's a good idea to have extras available for those who forget. You may also want to bring paper and additional Bibles.

Note that in many cases there will not be one "right" answer to the question. Answers will vary, especially when the group members are being asked to share their personal experiences.

STRUCTURING THE DISCUSSION TIME

You will need to determine with your group how long you want to meet each week so you can plan your time accordingly. Generally, most groups like to meet for either sixty minutes or ninety minutes, so you could use one of the following schedules:

Section	60 Minutes	90 Minutes
WELCOME (members arrive and get settled)	5 minutes	10 minutes
REFLECTION (discuss the opening question for the lesson)	10 minutes	15 minutes
DISCUSSION (discuss the Bible study questions in the Exploration and Reaction sections)	35 minutes	50 minutes
PRAYER/CLOSING (pray together as a group and dismiss)	10 minutes	15 minutes

As the group leader, it is up to you to keep track of the time and keep things moving along according to your schedule. You might want to set a timer for each segment so both you and the group members know when your time is up. (Note that there are some good phone apps for timers that play a gentle chime or other pleasant sound instead of a disruptive noise.) Don't feel pressured to cover every question you have selected if the group has a good discussion going. Again, it's not necessary to go around the circle and make everyone share.

Don't be concerned if the group members are silent or slow to share. People are often quiet when they are pulling together their ideas, and this might be a new experience for them. Just ask a question and let it hang in the air until someone shares. You can then say, "Thank you. What about others? What came to you when you reflected on the passage?"

GROUP DYNAMICS

Leading a group through *Life Lessons from 1, 2, 3 John and Jude* will prove to be highly rewarding both to you and your group members—but that doesn't mean you will not encounter any challenges along the way! Discussions can get off track. Group members may not be sensitive to the needs and ideas of others. Some might worry they will be expected to talk about matters that make them feel awkward. Others may express comments that result in disagreements. To help ease this strain on you and the group, consider the following ground rules:

- When someone raises a question or comment that is off the main topic, suggest you deal with it another time, or, if you feel led to go in that direction, let the group know you will be spending some time discussing it.
- If someone asks a question you don't know how to answer, admit it and move on. At your discretion, feel free to invite group members to comment on questions that call for personal experience.
- If you find one or two people are dominating the discussion time, direct a few questions to others in the group. Outside the main group time, ask the more dominating members to help you draw out the quieter ones. Work to make them a part of the solution instead of the problem.
- When a disagreement occurs, encourage the group members to process the matter in love. Encourage those on opposite sides to restate what they heard the other side say about the matter, and then invite each side to evaluate if that perception is accurate. Lead the group in examining other Scriptures related to the topic and look for common ground.

When any of these issues arise, encourage your group members to follow the words from the Bible: "Love one another" (John 13:34), "If it is possible, as far as it depends on you, live at peace with everyone" (Romans 12:18), and, "Be quick to listen, slow to speak and slow to become angry" (James 1:19).

Thank you again for taking the time to lead your group. May God reward your efforts and dedication and make your time together in this study fruitful for his kingdom.

ALSO AVAILABLE IN THE LIFE LESSONS SERIES

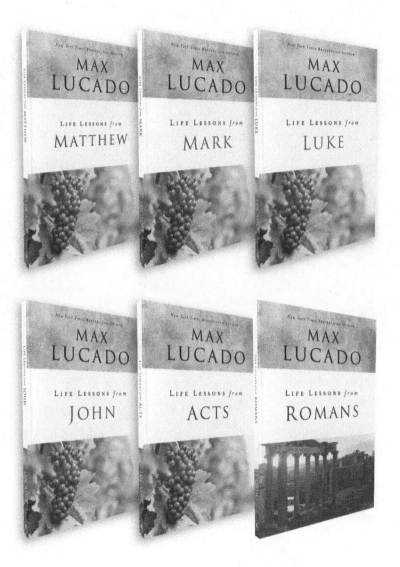

Now available wherever books and ebooks are sold.

ALSO AVAILABLE IN THE LIFE LESSONS SERIES

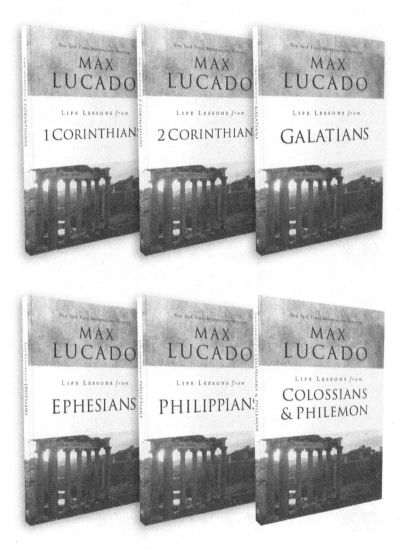

Now available wherever books and ebooks are sold.